INCUBI AND SUCCUBI

OR

DEMONIALITY

A TREATISE

wherein is shown that there are in existence on earth rational creatures besides man, endowed like him with a body and a soul, that are born and die like him, redeemed by our Lord Jesus-Christ, and capable of receiving salvation or damnation,

BY

THE REV. FATHER SINISTRARI OF AMENO

(17th century)

Published from the original Latin manuscript

discovered in London

in the year 1872,

and translated into French by

ISIDORE LISEUX

PREFACE TO THE FIRST EDITION

(Paris, 1875, in-80)

I was in London in the year 1872, and I hunted after old books: Car que faire là bas, à moins qu'on ne bouquine?[1] They caused me to live in past ages, happy to escape from the present, and to exchange the petty passions of the day for the peaceable intimacy of Aldus, Dolet or Estienne. One of my favourite booksellers was Mr Allen, a venerable old gentleman, whose place of business was in the Euston road, close to the gate of Regent's park. Not that his shop was particularly rich in dusty old books; quite the reverse: it was small, and yet never filled. Scarcely four or five hundred volumes at a time, carefully dusted, bright, arrayed with symmetry on shelves within reach of one's hand; the upper shelves remained unoccupied. On the right, Theology; on the left, the Greek and Latin Classics in a majority, with some French and Italian books; for such were Mr Allen's specialties : it seemed as if he absolutely ignored Shakespeare and Byron, and as if, in his mind, the literature of his country did not go beyond the sermons of Blair or Macculloch. What, at first sight, struck one most in those books, was the moderateness of their price, compared with their excellent state of preservation. They had evidently not been bought in a lot, at so much a cubic yard, like the rubbish of an auction, and yet the handsomest, the most ancient, the most venerable from their size, folios or quartos, were not marked higher than 2 or 3 shillings; an octavo was sold I shilling, the duodecimo six pence : each according to its size. Thus ruled Mr Allen, a methodical man, if ever there was one; and he was all the better for it, since, faithfully patronized by clergymen, scholars and collectors, he renewed his stock at a rate which more assuming speculators might have envied. But how did he get those well bound and well preserved volumes, forwhich, everywhere else, five or six times more would have been charged? Here also

---

[1] What can one do over there, unless he hunts up old books?

Mr Allen had his method, sure and regular. No one attended more assiduously the auctions which take place every day in London: his stand was marked at the foot of the auctioneer's desk. The rarest, choicest books passed before his eyes, contended for at often fabulous prices by Quaritch, Sotheran, Pickering, Toovey, and other bibliopolists of the British metropolis; Mr Allen smiled at such extravagance; when once a bid had been made by another, he would not add a penny, had an unknown Gutenberg or Valdarfer's Boccaccio been at stake. But if occasionally, through inattention or weariness, competition slackened (habent sua fata libelli), Mr Allen came forward: six pence!, he whispered, and sometimes the article was left him; sometimes even, two consecutive numbers, joined together for want of having separately met with a buyer, were knocked down to him, still for the minimum of six pence which was his maximum. Many of those slighted ones doubtless deserved their fate ; but among them might slip some that were not unworthy of the honours of the catalogue, and which, at any other time, buyers more attentive, or less whimsical might perhaps have covered with gold. This, however, did not at all enter into Mr Allen's calculation: the size was the only rule of his estimate. Now, one day when, after a considerable auction, he had exhibited in his shop purchases more numerous than usual, I especially noticed some manuscripts in the Latin language, the paper, the writing and the binding of which denoted an Italian origin, and which might well be two hundred years old. The title of one was, I believe : De Venenis; of another : De Viperis; of a third (the present work) : De Dæmonialitate, et Incubis, et Succubis. All three, moreover, by different authors, and independent of each other. Poisons, adders, demons, what a collection of horrors! yet, were it but for civility's sake, I was bound to buy something ; after some hesitation, I chose the last one : Demons, true, but Incubi, Succubi : the subject is not vulgar, and still less so the way in which it seemed to me to have been handled. In short, I had the volume for six-pence, a boon price for a quarto : Mr Allen doubtless deemed such a scrawl beneath the rate of type. That manuscript, on strong paper of the 17th century, bound in Italian parchment, and beautifully preserved, has 86 pages of text. The title and first page are in the author's hand, that of an old man ; the remainder is very distinctly written by another, but under his direction, as is testified by autographic side notes and rectifications distributed all through the work. It is therefore the genuine original manuscript, to all appearances unique and inedited. Our dealer in old books had purchased it a few days before at Sotheby's House, where had taken place (from the 6th to the 16th of December 1871) the sale of the books of baron Seymour Kirkup, an English collector, deceased in Florence. The manuscript was inscribed as follows on the sale catalogue : No 145. AMENO (R. P. Ludovicus Maria [Cotta] de). De Dæmonialitate, et Incubis, et Succubis, Manuscript. S c. XVII-XVIII. Who is that writer? Has he left printed works? That is a question I leave to bibliographers ; for, notwithstanding numerous investigations in special dictionaries, I have been unable to ascertain any thing on that score. Brunet (Manuel du libraire, art. COTTA d'Ameno) vaguely surmises his existence, but confuses him with his namesake, most likely also his fellow-townsman, Lazaro Agostino Cotta of Ameno, a barrister and literary man of Novara. "The author," says he, "whose real Christian names would seem to be Ludovico-Maria, has written many serious works..." The mistake is obvious. One thing is sure : our author was living in the last years of the 17th century, as appears from his own testimony, and had been a professor of Theology in Pavia. Be that as it may, his book has seemed to me most interesting in divers respects, and I confidently submit it to that select public for whom the invisible world is not a chimera. I should be much surprised if, after opening it at random, the reader was not tempted to retrace his steps and go on to the end. The philosopher, the confessor, the medical man will find therein, in conjunction with the robust faith of the middle ages, novel and ingenious views; the literary man, the curioso, will appreciate the solidity of reasoning, the clearness of style, the liveliness of recitals (for there are stories , and delicately told). All theologians have devoted more or less pages to the question of material intercourse between man and the demon; thick volumes have been written about witchcraft, and the merits of this work were but slender if it merely developed the ordinary thesis ; but such is not its characteristic. The ground-matter , from which it derives a truly original and philosophical stamp, is an entirely novel demonstration of the existence of Incubi and Succubi, as rational animals, both corporeal and spiritual like ourselves, living in our midst, being born and dying like us, and lastly redeemed, as we are, through the merits of Jesus-Christ, and capable of receiving salvation or damnation. In the Father of Ameno's opinion, those beings endowed with senses and reason, thoroughly distinct from Angels and Demons, pure spirits, are none other but the Fauns, Sylvans and Satyrs of paganism, continued by our Sylphs, Elfs and Goblins; and thus is connected anew the link of belief. On this score alone, not to mention the interest of details, this book has a claim to the attention of earnest readers : I feel convinced that attention will not be found wanting. I. L. May 1875. The foregoing advertisement was composed at the printer's, and ready for the press, when, strolling on the quays[2], I met by chance with a copy of the Index librorum prohibitorum. I mechanically opened it, and the first thing that struck my eyes was the following article : De Ameno Ludovicus Maria. Vide Sinistrari. My heart throbbed fast, I must confess. Was I at last on the trace of my author? Was it Demoniality that I was about to see nailed to the pillory of the Index? I flew to the last pages of the formidable volume, and read : SINISTRARI (Ludovicus Maria) de Ameno, De Delictis et P nis Tractatus absolutissimus. Donec corrigatur. Decret. 4 Martii 1709. Correctus autem juxta editionem Romanam anni 1753 permittitur. It was indeed he. The real name of the Father of Ameno was Sinistrai, and I was in possession of the title of one at least of those "serious works" which Brunet the bibliographer alluded to. The very title, De Delictis et P nis, was not unconnected with that of my

---

[2] Paris Embankment.

manuscript, and I had reason to presume that Demoniality was one of the offenses inquired into, and decided upon, by Father Sinistrari; in other words, that manuscript, to all appearances inedited, was perhaps published in the extensive work revealed to me ; perhaps even was it to that monography of Demoniality that the Tractatus de Delictis et P nis owed its condemnation by the Congregation of the Index. All those points required looking into. But it is necessary to have attempted investigations of that kind in order to appreciate the difficulties thereof. I consulted the catalogues of ancient books that came in my way ; I searched the back-shops of the dealers in old books, the antiquaries, as they say in Germany, addressing especially to the two or three firms who in Paris apply themselves to old Theology ; I wrote to the principal booksellers in London, Milan, Florence, Rome, Naples : all to no purpose ; the very name of Father Sinistrari of Ameno seemed to be unknown. I should perhaps have begun by enquiring at our National Library ; I was obliged to resort to it, and there at least I obtained an incipient gratification. I was shown two works by my author : a quarto of 1704, De incorrigibilium expulsione ab Ordinibus Regularibus, and the first tome of a set of his complete works : R. P. Ludovici Mariæ Sinistrari de Ameno Opera omnia (Romæ, in domo Caroli Giannini, 1753-1754, 3 vol. in-folio). Unfortunately that first tome contained but the Practica Criminalis Minorum illustrata ; De Delictis et P nis was the subject matter of the third tome, which, as well as the second, was missing at the Library. Yet, I had a positive indication, and I pursued my investigations. I might be more fortunate at the Library of St Sulpice Seminary. True, it is not open to the public ; but then, the Sulpician Fathers are hospitable : did they not of yore afford a refuge to repentant Des Grieux, and did not Manon Lescaut herself tread the flags of their parlour? I therefore ventured into the holy House ; it was half past twelve, dinner was nearly over ; I asked for the librarian, and after a few minutes, I saw coming to me a short old man, unexceptionably civil, who, leading me through the common parlour, introduced me into another much narrower, a mere cell, looking into a gallery and glazed full breadth, being thus exposed to every eye. An ingenious provision of which Des Grieux's escape had fully shown the urgency. I had no small trouble in explaining the object of my visit to the good Father, who was deaf and near sighted. He left me to go to the library, and soon returned, but empty handed : there also, in that sanctuary of Catholic Theology, Father Sinistrari of Ameno was entirely unknown. But one more expedient could I try : namely, to go to his brothers in St Francis, the Capuchin Fathers, in their convent of rue de la Santé! A cruel extremity, it will be granted, for I had but little chance of meeting there, as here, the lovely shadow of Manon. At last a letter from Milan put an end to my perplexity. The unfindable book was found ; I received at the same time the first edition of De Delictis et P nis (Venetiis, apud Hieronymum Albricium, 1700), and the edition of Rome, 1754. It was a complete treatise, tractatus absolutissimus, upon all imaginable crimes, offenses and sins ; but, let us hasten to say, in both those voluminous folios, Demoniality occupies scarcely five pages, without any difference in the text between the two editions. And those five pages are not even a summary of the manuscript work which I now give forth ; they only contain the proposition and conclusion (Nrs 1 to 27 and 112 to 115). As for that wherein lies the originality of the book, to wit the theory of rational animals, Incubi and Succubi, endowed like ourselves with a body and soul, and capable of receiving salvation and damnation, it were vain to look for it. Thus, after so many endeavours, I had settled all the points which I had intended to elucidate : I had discovered the identity of the Father of Ameno[3]; from the comparison of the two editions of De Delictis et P nis, the first condemned, the second allowed by the Congregation of the Index, I had gathered that the printed fragments of Demoniality had nothing to do with the condemnation of the book, since they had not been submitted to any correction ; lastly, I had become convinced that, save a few pages, my manuscript was absolutely inedited. A happy event of a

---

[3] Vide biographical notice at the end of this volume.

bibliographical Odyssey which I shall be excused for relating at length, for the "jollification" of bibliophiles "and none other".

ISIDORE LISEUX.

August 1875.

DEMONIALITY

OR

INCUBI AND SUCCUBI

The Latin Text to appear first on the left,

and the englished translation upon the right.

DÆMONIALITAS VOCABULUM Dæmonialiatis primo inventum reperio a Jo. Caramuele in sua Theologia fundamentali, nec ante illum inveni Auctorem, qui de hoc crimine tanquam distincto a Bestialitate locutus sit. Omnes enim Theologi Morales, secuti D. Thomam, 2.2., q. 154. in corp., sub specie Bestialitatis recensent omnem concubitum cum renon ejusdem speciei, ut ibi loquitur D. Thomas ; et proinde Cajetanus, in Commentario illius quæstionis et articuli, 2.2., q. 154., ad 3. dub., coitum cum Dæmone ponit in specie Bestialitatis ; et Cajetanum sequitur Silvester, vo Luxuria, Bonacina, de Matrim., q. 4., et alii.

DEMONIALITY

THE first author who, to my knowledge, invented the word Demoniality is John Caramuel, in his Fundamental Theology, and before him I find no one who distinguished that crime from Bestiality. Indeed, all Theological Moralists, following in the train of S. Thomas (2, 2, question 154), include, under the specific title of Bestiality, "every kind of carnal intercourse with any thing whatever of a different species" : such are the very words used by S. Thomas. Cajetanus, for instance, in his commentary on that question, classes intercourse with the Demon under the description of Bestiality ; so does Sylvester, de

2. Sed revera D. Thomas in illo loco considerationem non habuit ad coitum cum Dæmone : ut enim infra probabimus, hic coitus non potest in specie specialissima Bestialitatis comprehendi ; et ut veritati cohæreat sententia S. Doctoris, dicendum est , quod in citato loco, quando ait, quod peccatum contra naturam, alio modo si fiat per concubitum ad rem non ejusdem speciei, vocatur Bestialitas : sub nomine rei non ejusdem speciei intellexerit animal vivens, non ejusdem speciei cum homine:non enim usurpare potuit ibi nomen rei pro re, puta, ente communi ad animatum et inanimatum : si enim quis coiret cum cadavere humano, concubitum haberet ad rem non ejusdem speciei cum homine(maxime apud Thomistas, qui formam corporeitatis humanæ negant in cadavere), quod etiam esset si cadaveri bestiali copularetur ; et tamen talis coitus non esset bestialitas, sed mollities. Voluit igitur ibi D. Thomas præcise inteligere concubitum cum re vivente non ejusdem speciei cum homine, hoc est cum bruto, nullo autem modo comprehendere voluit coitum cum Dæmone.

Luxuria, Bonacina, de Matrimonio, question 4, and others. 2. However it is clear that in the above passage S. Thomas did not at all allude to intercourse with the Demon. As shall be demonstrated further on, that intercourse cannot be included in the very particular species of Bestiality ; and, in order to make that sentence of the holy Doctor tally with truth, it must be admitted that when saying of the unnatural sin, "that committed through intercourse with a thing of different species, it takes the name of Bestiality", S. Thomas, by a thing of different species, means a living animal, of another species than man : for he could not here use the word thing in its most general sense, to mean indiscriminately an animate or inanimate being. In fact, if a man should fornicate cum cadavere humano, he would have to do with a thing of a species quite different from his own (especially according to the Thomists, who deny the form of human corporeity in a corpse); similarly si cadaveri bestiali copularetur : and yet, talis coitus would not be bestiality, but pollution. What therefore S. Thomas intended here to specify with preciseness, is carnal intercourse with a

3. Coitus igitur cum Dæmone, sive Incubo, sive Succobo (qui proprie est Dæmonialitas), specie differt a Bestialitate, nec cum ea facit unam speciem specialissimam, ut opinatus est Cajetanus : peccata enim contra naturam specie inter se distingui contra opinionem nonnullorum Antiquorum , et Caramuelis, Summ., Armill., v. Luxur., n. 5., Jabien., eo. v. n. 6., Asten., lib. 2. tit. 46. art. 7., Caram. Theol. fundam. post Filliucium, et Crespinum a Borgia, est opinio communis ; et contraria est damnata in proposit.24.ex damnatis ab Alexandro VII.; tum quia singula continent peculiarem , et distinctam turpitudinem repugnantem castitati, et humanæ generationi ; tum quia quodlibet ex iis privat bono aliquo secundum naturam, et institutionem actus venerei, ordinati ad finem generationis humanæ ; tum quia quodlibet ipsorum habet diversum motivum, per se sufficiens ad privandum eodem bono diversimode, ut optime philosophatur Filliuc., tom. 2. c. 8. tract. 3o. q. 3. No 142; Cresp., q. mor. sel. contro.; Caramuel., q. 5. per tot.

living thing of a species different from man, that is to say, with a beast, and he never in the least thought of intercourse with the Demon. 3. Therefore, intercourse with the Demon, whether Incubus or Succubus (which is, properly speaking, Demoniality), differs in kind from Bestiality, and does not in connexion with it form one very particular species, as Cajetanus wrongly gives it; for, whatever may have said to the contrary some Ancients, and later Caramuel in his Fundamental Theology, unnatural sins differ from each other most distinctly. Such at least is the general doctrine, and the contrary opinion has been condemned by Alexander VII: first, because each of those sins carries with itself its peculiar and distinct disgrace, repugnant to chastity and to human generation; secondly, because the commission thereof entails each time the sacrifice of some good by its nature attached to the institution of the venereal act, the normal end of which is human generation; lastly, because they each have a different motive which in itself is sufficient to bring about, in divers ways, the deprivation of the same good, as has been

4. Ex his autem infertur, quod etiam Dæmonialitas specie differt a Bestialitate : singula enim ipsarum peculiarem et distinctam turpitudinem, castitati ac humanæ generationi repugnantem, involvit;siquidem Bestialitas est copula cum bruto vivente, ac sensibus et motu proprio prædito : Dæmonialitas autem est commixtio cum cadavere (stando in sententia communi, quam infra examinabimus), nec sensum, nec motum vitalem habente; et per accidens est, quod a Dæmone moveatur. Quod si immunditia commissa cum brutali cadavere, vel humano, differt specie a Sodomia et Bestialitate, ab ista differt pariter specie etiam Dæmonialitas, in qua, juxta communem sententiam, homo cum cadavere concumbit accidentaliter moto. 5. Et confirmatur : quia in peccatis contra naturam, seminatio innaturalis (hoc est, ea ad quam regulariter non potest sequi generatio) habet rationem generis ; subjectum vero talis seminationis est differentia constituens species, sub tali genere : unde si seminatio fiat in terram, aut corpus inamine, est mollities; si fiat cum homine in

clearly shown by Fillucius, Crespinus and Caramuel. 4. It follows that Demoniality differs in kind from Bestiality, for each has its peculiar and distinct disgrace, repugnant to chastity and human generation. Bestiality is connexion with a living beast, endowed with its own peculiar senses and impulses ; Demoniality, on the contrary, is copulation with a corpse (according at least to the general doctrine which shall be considered hereafter), a senseless and motionless corpse which is but accidentally moved through the power of the Demon. Now, if fornication with the corpse of a man, a woman, or a beast differs in kind from Sodomy and Bestiality, there is the same difference with regard to Demoniality, which, according to general opinion, is the intercourse of man with a corpse accidentally set in motion. 5. Another proof : in sins against nature, the unnatural semination (which cannot be regularly followed by generation) is a genus; but the object of such semination is the difference which marks the species under the genus. Thus, whether semination takes place on the ground, or on an inanimate body, it is pollution; if vase præpostero, est Sodomia ; si fiat cum bruto, est bestialitas : quæ absque controversia inter se specie differunt , eo quod terra, seu cadaver, homo, et brutum, quæ sunt subjecta talis seminationis, specie differunt inter se. Sed Dæmon a bruto non solum differt specie, sed plusquam specie : differunt enim per corporeum, et incorporeum, quæ sunt differentiæ genericæ. Sequitur ergo quod seminationes factæ cum aliis differunt inter se specie, quod est intentum. 6. Pariter, trita est doctrina Moralistarum fundata in Tridentino,sess. 14, c. 5. D. Th. in 4. dist. 16. q. 3. art. 2., Vasquez, q. 91. art. I. dub. 2. n. 6., Reginald. Valenz,. Medin. Zerola. Pesant. Sajir, Sott. Pitig. Henriquez apud Bonac.de Sac. disp. 5. q. 5. sect. 2. punct. 2.§ 3. diffic. 3. n. 5., et tradita per Theologos , quod in confessione manifestandæ sint tantum circumstantiæ quæ mutant speciem peccatorum.Si igitur Dæmonialitas et Bestialitas sunt ejusdem speciei specialissimæ , sufficit in confessione dicere : Bestialitatis peccatum commisi, quantumvis confitens cum Dæmone cum homine in vase præpostero, it is Sodomy; with a beast, bestiality : crimes which unquestionably all differ from each other in species, just as the ground, the corpse, the man and the beast, passive objects talis seminationis, differ in species from each other. But the difference between the Demon and the beast is not only specific, it is more than specific : the nature of the one is corporeal, of the other incorporeal, which makes a generic difference. Whence it follows that seminationes practised on different objets differ in species from each other : and that is substantiated. 6. It is also a trite doctrine with Moralists, established by the Council of Trent, session 14, and admitted by Theologians, that in confession it suffices to state the circumstances which alter the species of sins. If therefore Demoniality and Bestiality belonged to the same very particular species, it would be enough that, each time he has fornicated with the Demon, the penitent should say to his confessor : I have been guilty of the sin of Bestiality. But that is not so : therefore those two sins do not both belong to the same very particular species.

concubuerit. Hoc autem falsum est : igitur non sunt ejusdem speciei specialissimæ. 7. Quod si dicatur, aperidum esse in confessione circumstantiam concubitus cum Dæmone ratione peccati contra Religionem : peccatum contra Religionem committitur, aut ex cultu, aut ex reverentia, aut ex deprecatione, aut ex pacto, aut ex societate cum Dænibe (D. Thomas, 2. 2. q. 90. art. 2. et q. 95. art. 4. in corp.) ; sed, ut infra dicemus, dantur Succubi, et Incubi, quibus nullum prædictorum exhibetur, et tamen copula sequitur : igitur respectu istorum nulla intervenit irreligiositas, et commixtio cum istis nullam habebit rationem ulteriorem, quam puri et simplicis coitus, qui, si est ejusdem speciei cum Bestialitate, sufficienter exprimetur dicendo: Bestialitatem commisi ; quod tamen falsum est. 8. Ulterius in confesso est apud omnes Theologos Morales, quod longe gravior est copula cum Dæmone, quam cum quolibet bruto ; in eadem autem specie specialissima peccati, non datur unum peccatum gravius atero, sed omnia æque gravia sunt;

7. It may be urged that if the circumstances of a sensual intercourse with the Demon should be revealed to the Confessor, it is on account of its offense against Religion, an offense which comes either from the worship rendered to the Demon, or from the homage or prayers offered up to him, or from the compact of fellowship entered into with him (S. Thomas, quest. 90). But, as will be seen hereafter, there are Incubi and Succubi to whom none of the foregoing applies, and yet copula sequitur. There is consequently,in that special case, no element of irreligion, no other character quam puri et simplicis coitus; and, if of the same species as Bestiality, it would be adequately stated by saying : I have been guilty of the sin of Bestiality; which is not so. 8. Besides, it is acknowledged by all Theological Moralists that copula cum Dæmone is much more grievous than the same act committed with any beast soever. Now, in the same very particular species of sins, one sin is not more grievous than

perinde enim est coire cum cane, aut asina, aut equa ; sequitur ergo, quod si Dæmonialitas est gravior Bestialitate, non sint ambo ejusdem speciei. Nec dicendum gravitatem majorem in Dæmonialitate petendam esse ab irreligiositate, seu superstitione ex societate cum Dæmone, ut scribit Cajetanus ad 2. 2. q. 154., ar. 11.§ ad 3. in fine, quia hoc fallit in aliquibus Succubis et Incubis, ut supra dictum est ; tum quia gravitas major statuitur in Dæmonialitate præ Bestialitate, in genere vitii contra naturam : major autem gravitas in illa supra istam ratione irreligiositatis exorbitat ex illo genere, proinde non facit in illo genere, et ex se graviorem. 9. Statura igitur differentia specifica Dæmonialitatis a Bestialitate, ut gravitas illius percipiatur in ordine ad pænem de quæ principaliter nobis tractandum est, est necessarium inquirere quotupliciter Dæmonialitas accidat. Non desunt qui sibi nimis scioli negant quod gravissimi Auctores scripsere, et quod quotidiana constant experientia, Dæmonem scilicet tum Incubum, tum Succubum, non solum hominibus, sed etiam brutis carnaliter conjungi. Aiunt another; all are equally so : it comes to the same whether connection is had with a bitch, an ass, or a mare ; whence it follows that if Demoniality is more grievous than Bestiality, those two acts are not of the same species. And let it not be argued, with Cajetanus, that Demoniality is more grievous on account of the offense to religion from the worship rendered to the Demon or the compact of fellowship entered into with him : as has been shown above, that is not always met with in the connection of man with Incubi and Succubi ; moreover, if in the genus of unnatural sin Demoniality is more grievous than Bestiality, the offense to Religion is quite foreign to that aggravation, since it is foreign to that genus itself. 9. Now, having laid down the specific difference between Demoniality and Bestiality, so that the gravity thereof may be duly appreciated in view of the penalty to be inflicted (and that is our most essential object), we must inquire in how many different ways the sin of Demoniality may be committed. There is no lack of people who, infatuated with their small baggage of knowledge, venture to deny what has been written by the gravest authors proinde esse hominum imaginationem, phantasmatibus a Dæmone pertubatis læsam, seu dæmoniaca esse præstigia : sucuti etiam Sagæ, seu Striges, sola imaginatione perturbata a Dæmone , sibi videntur assistere ludis, choreis, conviviis, et conventibus nocturnis, et carnaliter Dæmoni commisceri ; nullo vero reali modo deferuntur corpore ad ejusmodi loca et actiones, prout textualiter dicitur in quodam Capitulo, ac duobus Conciliis. Cap. Episcop. 26. q. 5., Conc. Ancyr. c. 24., Conc. Rom. 4. sub Damaso, c. 5. apud Laur. Epitom. vo. Saga. 10. Sed non negatur, quin aliquando mulierculæ, illusæe a Dæmonibus, videantur nocturnis Sagarum ludis corporaliter interesse, dum tamen sola imaginaria visione ipsis hoc accidit : sicut etiam in somnis videtur nonnullis cum fæmina aliqua concumbere, et semen vere excernitur, non tamen concubitus ille realis est , sed tantum phantasticus, paratus non raro per illusionem diabolicam ; et in hoc verissimum est quod habent citatum Capitulum et Concilia.

and is testified by every day experience : namely, that the Demon, whether Incubus or Succubus, unites carnally not only with men and women, but also with beasts. They allege that it all comes from the human imagination troubled by the craft of the Demon, and that there is nothing in it but phantasmagoria and diabolical spells. The like happens, they say, to Witches or Sagas, who, under the influence of an illusion brought on by the Demon, fancy that they attend the nightly sports, dances, revels and vigils, and have carnal intercourse with the Demon, though in reality they are not bodily transferred to those places nor taking part in those deeds, as has been defined verbatim by a Capitule and two Councils. 10. Of course, it is not contested that sometimes young women, deceived by the Demon, fancy taking part, in their flesh and blood, in the nightly vigils of Witches, without its being any thing but an imaginary vision. Thus, in a dream, one sometimes fancies cum f mina aliqua concumbere, et semen vere excernitur, non tamen concubitus ille realis est, but merely fantastic, and often brought about by a diabolical illusion : and here the above mentioned Capitule and

Sed hoc non semper est ; sed ut in pluribus, corpore deferuntur Sagæ ad ludos nocturnos, et vere carnaliter corpore conjunguntur Dæmoni, et Malefici non minus Dæmoni succubo miscentur, et hæc est sententia Theologorum, et jure consultorum Catholicorum, quos abunde citat Frater Franciscus Maria Guaccius in suo libro intitulato Compendium Maleficarum; Grilland. Remig. Petr. Damian. Sylvest. Alphon. a Cast. Abul. Cajet. Senon. Crespet. Spine. Anan. apud Guaccium, Comp. Maleaf., c. 15. § Altera, quam verissimam... n. 69. lib. p.; quæ sententia confirmatur decem et octo exemplis ibidem allatis et relatis per viros doctos et veridicos de quorum fide ambigendum non est, quibus probatur Maleficos et Sagas corporaliter ad ludos convenire, et cum Dæmonibus succubis et incubis corporaliter turpissime commisceri. Et pro omnibus sufficere debet auctoritas Divi Augustini, qui loquens de concubitu hominum cum Dæmonibus, sic ait lib. 15. de Civitate Dei, c. 23.: "Et quoniam creberrima fama est, multique se expertos, vel ab eis qui experti essent, de quorum fide dubitandum non est, audivisse confirmant, Sylvanos et Faunos, quos vulgo Incubos vocant, improbos sæpe extitisse mulieribus, et earum appetiisse et peregisse

Councils are perfectly right. But this is not always the case ; on the contrary, it more often happens that Witches are bodily present at nightly vigils and have with the Demon a genuine carnal and corporeal connection, and that likewise Wizards copulate with the Succuba or female Demon. Such is the opinion of Theologians as well as of jurists, whose names will be found at length in the Compendium Maleficarum, or Chronicle of Witches, by Brother Francis Marie Guaccius. This doctrine is therein confirmed by eighteen instances adduced from the recitals of learned and truthful men whose testimony is beyond suspicion, and which prove that Wizards and Witches are indeed bodily present at vigils and most shamefully copulate with Demons, Incubi or Succubi. And, after all, to settle the question, we have the authority of S. Austin, who, speaking of carnal intercourse between men and the Demon, expresses himself as follows, book 15th, chapt. 23d of the City of God : "It is widely credited, and such belief is confirmed by the direct or indirect testimony of thoroughly trustworthy people, that Sylvans and Fauns, commonly called Incubi, have frequently molested women, sought and obtained from concubitum. Et quosdam Dæmones, quos Dusios Galli nuncupant, hanc assidue immunditiam et tentare et efficere, plures talesque asseverant, ut hoc negare impudentia videatur." Hæ Augustinus. II. Prout autem apud diversos Auctores legitur, et pluribus experimentis comprobatur, duplici modo Dæmon hominibus carnaliter copulatur : uno modo quo Maleficis et Sagis jungitur, alio modo quo aliis hominibus minime maleficis miscetur. 12. Quantum ad primum modum, non copulatur Dæmon Sagis, seu Maleficis, nisi præmissa solemni professione, qua iniquissimi homines Dæmoni addicuntur ; quæ professio, ut ex variis Auctoribus referentibus confessiones Sagarum judiciales in tormentis factas, quas collegit Franciscus Maria Guaccius, Comp. Malef, c. 7., lib. I., consistit in undecim ceremoniis : 13. Primo, ineunt pactum expressum cum Dæmone, aut alio Mago seu Malefico vicem them coition. There are even Demons, whom the Gauls call Duses or Elfs, who very regularly indulge in those unclean practices : the fact is testified by so many and such weighty authorities, that it were impudent to doubt it." Such are the very words of S. Austin. 11. Now, several authors profess, and it is confirmed by numerous experiments, that the Demon has two ways of copulating carnally with men or women : the one which it uses with Witches or Wizards, the other with men or women entirely foreign to witchcraft. 12. In the first case, the Demon does not copulate with Witches or Wizards until after a solemn profession, in virtue of which such wretched human beings yield themselves up to him.According to several authors who have related the judicial admissions of Witches when on the rack, and whose recitals have been collected by Francis-Marie Guaccius, Compend. Malef., book 1, chapt. 7, that profession consists of eleven ceremonials : 13. Firstly, the Novices have to conclude with the Demon, or some other Wizard or

Dæmonis gerente, et testibus præsentibus, de servitio diabolico suscipiendo : Dæmon vero vice versa honores, divitias, et carnales delectationes illis pollicetur. Guacc. loc. cit. fol. 34. 14. Secundo, abnegant catholicam fidem, subducunt se obedientiæ Dei, renuntiant Christo, et protectioni Beatissimæ Virginis Mariæ, ac Ecclesiæ omnibus sacramentis. Guacc., loc. cit. 15. Tertio, projiciunt a se Coronam, seu Rosarium B.V.M., Chordam S.P.Francisci, aut Corrigiam S. Augustini, aut Scapulare Carrmelitarum, si quod habent, Crucem, Medaleas, Agnos Dei, et quidquid sacri aut benedicti gestabant, et pedibus ea proculcant. Guacc. loc. cit. fol. 35. Grilland. 16. Quarto, vovent in manibus Diaboli obedientiam, et subjectionem, eique præstant homagium et vassallagium, tangendo quoddam volumen nigerrimum. Spondent, quod nunquam redibunt ad fidem Christi, nec Dei præcepta servabunt, nec ulla bona opera facient, sed ad sola mandata Dæmonis

Magician acting in the Demon's place, an express compact by which, in the presence of witnesses, they enlist in the Demon's service, he giving them in exchange his pledge for honours, riches and carnal pleasures. 14. Secondly, they abjure the catholic faith, withdraw from the obedience to God, renounce Christ and the protection of the most blessed Virgin Mary, and all the Sacraments of the Church. 15. Thirdly, they cast away the Crown, or Rosary of the most blessed Virgin Mary, the girdle of S. Francis, or the strap of S. Austin, or the scapular of the Carmelites, should they belong to one of those Orders, the Cross, the Medals, the Agnus Dei, whatever other holy or consecrated object may have been about their person, and trample them all underfoot. 16. Fourthly, in the hands of the Devil they vow obedience and subjection; they pay him homage and vassalage, laying their fingers on some very black book. They bind themselves never to return to the faith of Christ, to observe none of the divine precepts, to do no good work, but attendent, et ad conventus nocturnos diligenter accedent. Guacc. loc. cit. fol. 36. 17. Quinto, spondent se enixe curaturos, et omni studio ac sedulitate procuraturos adducere alios mares et fæminas ad suam sectam, et cultum Dæmonis. Guacc. loc. cit. 18. Sexto, baptizantur a Diabolo sacrilego quodam baptismo, et abnegatis Patrinis et Matrinis baptismi Chirsti, et Confirmationis, et nomine, quod sibi fuit primo impositum, a Diabolo sibi assignantur Patrinus et Matrina novi, qui ipsos instruant in arte maleficiorum, et imponitur nomen novum, quod plerumque scurrile est. Guacc.loc. cit. 19. Septimo, abscindunt partem propriorum indumentorum, et illam offerunt Diabolo in signum homagii, et Diabolus illam asportat,et servat.Guacc.loc.cit.fol.38. 20. Octavo, format Diabolus circulum super terram, et in eo stantes Novitii Malefici et Sagæ firmant juramento omnia, quæ ut dictum est promiserunt. Guacc. loc. cit.

to obey the Demon alone and, to attend diligently the nightly conventicles. 17. Fifthly, they promise to strive with all their power, and to give their utmost zeal and care for the enlistment of other males and females in the service of the Demon. 18. Sixthly, the Devil administers to them a kind of sacrilegious baptism, and after abjuring their Godfathers and Godmothers of the Baptism of Christ and Confirmation, they have assigned to them a new Godfather and a new Godmother, who are to instruct them in the arts of witchcraft ; they drop their former name and exchange it for another, more frequently a scurrilous nickname. 19. Seventhly, they cut off a part of their own garments, and tender it as a token of homage to the Devil, who takes it away and keeps it. 20. Eighthly, the Devil draws on the ground a circle wherein stand the Novices, Witches and Wizards, and there they confirm by oath all their aforesaid promises.

21. Nono, petunt a Diabolo deleri a libro Christi, et describi in libro suo, et profertur liber nigerrimus, quem tetigerunt præstando homagium, ut dictum est supra, et ungue Diaboli in eo exarantur. Guacc. loc. cit. 22. Decimo, promittunt Diabolo statis temporibus sacrificia, et oblationes ; singulis quindecim diebus, vel singulo mense saltem, necem alicujus infantis, aut mortale veneficium, et singulis hebdomadis alia mala in damnum humani generis, ut grandines, tempestates, incendia, mortem animalum, etc. Guacc. loc. cit. fol. 40.. 23. Undecimo, sigillantur a Dæmone aliquo charactere, maxime ii, de quorum constantia dubitat. Character vero non est semper ejusdem formæ, aut figuræ : aliquando enim est simile lepori, aliquando pedi bufonis, aliquando araneæ, vel catello, vel gliri; imprimitur autem in locis corporeis magis occultis : viris quidem aliquando sub palpebris, aliquando sub axillis, aut labiis, aut humeris, aut sede ima, aut alibi; mulieribus autem plerumque in mammis, aut locis muliebribus. Porro sigillum, quo talis signa imprimuntur, est unquis Diaboli. Quibus peractis ad instructionem

21. Ninthly, they request the Devil to strike them out of the book of Christ, and to inscribe them in his own. Then comes forth that very black book on which, as has been said before, they laid hands when doing homage, and they are inscribed therein with the Devil's claw. 22. Tenthly, they promise the Devil sacrifices and offerings at stated times : once a fortnight or at least each month, the murder of some child, or an homicidal act of sorcery, and other weekly misdeeds to the prejudice of mankind, such as hailstorms, tempests, fires, cattle plagues, etc. 23. Eleventhly, the Demon imprints on them some mark, especially on those whose constancy he suspects. That mark, moreover, is not always of the same shape or figure: sometimes it is the image of a hare, sometimes a toad's leg, sometimes a spider, a puppy, a dormouse. It is imprinted on the most hidden parts of the body : with men, under the eye-lids, or the armpits, or the lips, on the shoulder, the fundament, or somewhere else ; with women, it is usually on the breasts or the privy parts. Now, the stamp which imprints those marks is none other but the Devil's claw. This having

Magistrorum qui Novitios initiarunt, hi promittunt denuo, se nunquam Eucharistiam adoraturos ; injuriosos Sanctis omnibus, et maxime B. V. M. futuros ; conculcaturos ac conspurcaturos Sacras Imagines, Crucem, ac Sanctorum Reliquias; nunquam usuros Sacramentis, aut sacramentalibus, nisi ad maleficia ; integram confessionem sacramentalem sacerdoti nunquam facturos, et suum cum Dæmone commercium semper celaturos. Et Diabolus vicissim pollicetur, se illis semper præsto futurm ; se in hoc mundo votis eorum satifacturum, et post mortem illos esse beaturum. Sic peracta professione solemni, assignatur singulis eorum Diabolus, qui appellatur Magistellus, cum quo in partes secedunt, et carnaliter commiscentur : ille quidem in specie fæminæ, si initiatus est vir ; in forma autem viri, et aliquando satyri, aliquando hirci, si fæmina est saga professa. Guacc. loc. cit. fol. 42 et 43. 24. Quod su qæratur ab Auctoribus, quomodo possit Dæmon, qui corpus non habet, corporalem commixtionem habere cum homine : respondent communiter, been all performed in accordance with the instructions of the Teachers who have initiated the Novices, these promise lastly never to worship the Eucharist; to insult all Saints and especially the most blessed Virgin Mary; to trample under foot and vilify the holy images, the Cross and the relics of Saints ; never to use the sacraments or sacramental ceremonials; never to make a full confession to the priest, but to keep always hidden from him their intercourse with the Demon. The Demon, in exchange, engages to give them always prompt assistance; to fulfil their desires in this world and to make them happy after their death. The solemn profession being thus performed, each has assigned to himself a Devil, called Magistellus or Assistant Master, with whom he retires in private for carnal satisfaction; the said Devil being, of course, in the shape of a woman if the initiated person is a man, in the shape of a man, sometimes of a satyr, sometimes of a buck-goat, if it is a woman who has been received a witch. 24. If the authors be asked how it comes to pass that the Demon, who has no body, yet has carnal intercourse with man or woman, they unanimously answer that quod Dæmon aut assumit alterius maris aut fæminæ, juxta exigentiam, cadaver, aut ex mixtione aliarum materiarum effingit sibi corpus, quod movet, et mediante quo homini unitur. Et subdut, quod quando fæminæ gaudent imprægnari a Dæmone (quod non fit, nisi in gratiam fæminarum hoc optantium), Dæmon se transformat in succubam, et juncta homini semen ab eo recipit ; aut per illusionem nocturnam in somnis procurat ab homine pollutionem, et semen prolectum in suo nativo calore et cum vitali spiritu conservant, et incubando fæminæ infert in ipsius matricem, ex quo sequitur conceptio. Ita multis citatis docent Guaccius, l. I. c.12., per totum, qui prædicta multis exemplis desumptis a variis Doctoribus confirmat. 25. Alio modo jungitur Dæmon tum Incubus, tum Succubus, hominibus, fæminis aut maribus, a quibus nec honorem, nec sacrificia, oblationes, maleficia, quæ a Sagis et Maleficis, ut supra dictum est, præ tendit, recipit ; sed ostendens deperdite amorem, nil aliud appetit, quam carnaliter commisceri cum iis quos amat. Multa the Demon assumes the corpse of another human being, male or female as the case may be, or that, from the mixture of other materials, he shapes for himself a body endowed with motion, and by means of which he is united with the human being; and they add that when women are desirous of becoming pregnant by the Demon (which only occurs by the consent and express wish of the said women), the Demon is transformed into a Succuba, et juncta homini semen ab eo recipit; or else he procures pollution from a man during his sleep, et semen prolectum in suo nativo calore, et cum vitali spiritu conservat, et incubando f minæ infert in ipsius matricem, whence follows impregnation. Such is the teaching of Guaccius, book I, chapt. 12, who supports it on a number of quotations and instances taken from various Doctors.

25. At other times also the Demon, whether Incubus or Succubus, copulates with men or women from whom he receives none of the sacrifices, homage or offerings which he is wont to exact from Wizards or Witches, as aforesaid. He is then but a passionate lover, having only one desire : the carnal possession of the

sunt de hoc exempla, quæ ab Auctoribus referuntur, ut Menippi Lycii, qui fuit sollicitatus a quadam fæmina ad sibi nubendum, postquam cum ea multoties coivit ; et detecta fæmina quænam esset a quodam Philospho, qui convivio nuptiali intererat, et Menippo dixit illam esse Compusam, puta Dæmonem succubam, statim ejulans evanuit, ut narrat Coelius Rhodiginus, Antiq., lib. 29. c. 5. Pariter adolescens quidam Scotus a Dæmone succuba omnium gratissima, quas vidisset, forma, quæa occlusis cubiculi foribus ad se ventitabat, blanditiis, osculis, amplexibus per multos menses fuit sollicitatus,ut secum coiret, ut scribit Hector Boethius, Hist. Scotor. lib. 8., quod tamen a casto juvene obtinere non potuit. 26. Similiter, multas fæminas legimus ab Incubo Dæmone expetitas ad coitum, ipsisque repugnantibus facinus admittere, precibus, fletibus, blanditiis, non secus ac perditissimus amasius, procurasse animum ipsarum demulcere, et ad congressum inclinare ; et quamvis aliquoties hoc eveniat loved ones. Of this there are numerous instances to be found in the authors, amongst which the case of Menippus Lycius, who, after frequent coition with a woman, was by her entreated to marry her; but a certain philosopher, who partook of the wedding entertainment, having guessed what that woman was, told Menippus that he had to deal with a Compusa, that is a Succuba Demon ; whereupon the bride vanished bewailing : such is the narrative given by C lius Rhodiginus, Antiq., book 29, chapt. 5. Hector Boethius (Hist. Scot.) also relates the case of a young Scot, who, during many months, with closed doors and windows, was visited in his bed-room by a Succuba Demon of the most bewitching beauty ; caresses, kisses, embraces, entreaties, she resorted to every blandishment ut secum coiret : but she could not prevail on the chaste young man. 26. We read likewise of numerous women incited to coition by the Incubus Demon, and who, though reluctant at first of yielding to him, are soon moved by his entreaties, tears and endearments; he is a desperate lover and must not be denied. And although this comes sometimes of the craft of some ob maleficium, ut nempe Dæmon missus a maleficis hoc procuret : tamen non raro Dæmon ex se hoc agit, ut scribit Guaccius, Comp. Mal. lib. 3. c. 8., et non solum hoc evenit cum mulieribus, sed etiam cum equabus, cum quibus commiscetur ; quæ si libenter coitum admittunt, ab eo curantur optime, ac ipsarum jubæ varie artificiosis et inextricabilibus nodis texuntur ; si autem illum adversentur, eas male tractat, percutit, macras reddit, et tandem necat, ut quotidiana constat experientia. 27. Et quod mirum est, et pene incapabile, tales Incubi, qui Italice vocantur Folleti, Hispanice Duendes, Gallice Follets, nec Exorcistis obediunt, nec exorcismos pavent, nec res sacras reverentur ad earum approximationem timorem ostendendo, sicuti faciunt Dæmones, qui obsessos vexant ; quantumvis enim maligni Spiritus sint obstinati, nec parere velint Exorcistæ præcipienti, ut exeant a corporibus quæ obsident, tamen ad prolationem Sanctissimi Nominis Jesu, aut Mariæ, aut aliquorum versuum Sacræ Scripturæ, impositionem Reliquiarum, maxime Ligni Sanctæ Crucis, approximationem Sacrarum Imaginum, ad os obsessi rugiunt, strident, frendent, concutiuntur, et timorem

Wizard who avails himself of the agency of the Demon, yet the Demon not infrequently acts on his own account; and it happens not merely with women, but also with mares; if they readily comply with his desire, he pets them, and plaits their mane in elaborate and inextricable tresses; but if they resist, he ill-treats and strikes them, smites them with the glanders, and finally puts them to death, as is shown by daily experience. 27. A most marvellous and well nigh incomprehensible fact : the Incubi whom the Italians call Folletti, the Spaniards Duendes, the French Follets, do not obey the Exorcists, have no dread of exorcisms, no reverence for holy things, at the approach of which they are not in the least overawed; very different in that respect from the Demons who vex those whom they possess; for, however obstinate those evil Spirits may be, however restive to the injunctions of the Exorcist who bids them leave the body they possess, yet, at the mere utterance of the most holy name of Jesus or Mary, or of some verses of Holy Writ, at the mere imposition of relics, especially of a piece of the wood of the Holy Cross, or ac horrorem ostendunt. Folleti vero nihil horum, ut dictum est, ostendut, nec a divexatione, nisi post longum tempus, cessant. Hujus rei testis sum oculatus, et historiam recito quæ reipsa humanam fidem superat : sed testis mihi sit Deus quod puram veritatem multorum testimonio comprobatam describo. 28. Virginti quinque abhinc annis, plus minusve, dum essem Lector Sacræ Theologiæ in Conventu Sanctæ Crucis Papiæ, reperiebatur in illa civitate honesta quædam foemina maritata optimæ conscientiæ, et bonum habens ab omnibus eam agnoscentibus, maxime Religiosis, testimonium, quæ vocabatur Hieronyma ; et habitabat in parochia Sancti Michaelis. Hæc quadam die domi suæ panem pinserat, et per furmarium miserat ad illum decoquendum. Reportat panes coctos furnarius, et cum illis grandem quamdam placentam curiose elaboratam, conditam butyro, et pastulis Venetis, ut in ea civitate solent fieri placentæ hujusmodi. Renuit illa placentam recipere, dicens se talem nullam fecisse. Replicat furnarius, se illa die alium panem the sight of the holy images, they roar at the mouth of the possessed person, they gnash, shake, quiver, and display fright and awe. But the Folletti show none of those signs, and leave off their vexations but after a long space of time. Of this I was an eye-witness, and shall relate a story which verily passes human belief : but I take God to witness that I tell the precise truth, corroborated by the testimony of numerous persons. 28. About twenty five years ago, when I was a lecturer on Sacred Theology in the convent of the Holy Cross, in Pavia, there was living in that city a married woman of unimpeachable morality, and who was most highly spoken of by all such as knew her, especially by the Friars; her name was Hieronyma, and she lived in the parish of S. Michael. One day, this woman had kneaded bread at home and given it out to bake. The oven-man brought her back her loaves when baked, and with them a large cake of a peculiar shape, and made of butter and Venetian paste, as is usual in that city. She declined to take it in, saying she had not made any thing of the kind. -- "But" , said the oven-man, "I had no other bread" but yours to bake to-day, therefore this coquendum non habuisse, nisi illum quem ab ea habuerat ; oportere proinde, etiam placentam a se fuisse factam, licet minime de illa recordaretur. Acquievit foemina, et placentam cum viro suo, filia quam habebat triennem, et famula comedit. Sequenti nocte dum cubaret mulier cum viro suo, et ambo dormirent, expergefacta est a quadam tenuissima voce, velut acutissimi sibili ad ipsius aures susurrante, verbis tamen distinctis : interrogavit autem foeminam, num placenta illi placuisset? Pavens f mina c pit se munire signo Crucis, et invocare sæpius nomina Jesu et Mariæ. Replicabat vox, ne paveret, se nolle illi nocere, immo quæcumque illi placerent paratum exsequi, esse filo captum pulchritudinis suæ, et nil amplius desiderare, quam ejus amplexu frui. Tum f mina sensit aliquem suaviantem ipsius genas, sed tactus ita levis, ac mollis, ac si esset gossipium subtilissime carminatum id a quo tacta fuit. Respuit illa invitantem, nec ullum responsum illi dedit : sed jugiter nomen Jesu et Mariæ repetebat, et se Crucis signo muniebat ; et sic per spatium quasi horæ dimidiæ tentata fuit, et postea abscessit tentator. Sequenti mane fuit mulier ad confessarium virum prudentem ac doctum, a quo cake also must have come from your house; your memory is at fault". The good lady allowed herself to be persuaded, and partook of the cake with her husband, her little girl three years old, and the house servant. The next night, whilst in bed with her husband, and both asleep, she suddenly woke up at the sound of a very slender voice, something like a shrill hissing, whispering in her ears, yet with great distinctness, and inquiring whether "the cake had been to her taste?" The good lady, frightened, set about guarding herself with a sign of the cross and repeatedly calling the names of Jesus and Mary. "Be not afraid," said the voice, "I mean you no harm ; quite the reverse : I am prepared to do any thing to please you; I am captivated by your beauty, and desire nothing more than to enjoy your embraces" . And she felt somebody kissing her cheeks, so lightly, so softly, that she might have fancied being grazed by the finest down. She resisted without giving any answer, merely repeating over and over again the names of Jesus and Mary, and crossing herself ; the tempter kept on thus for nearly half an hour, when he withdrew. The next morning the dame called on her Confessor, a discreet and learned man, fuit in fide confirmata et exhortata, ut viriliter, sicut fecerat, resisteret, et sacris Reliquiis se muniret. Sequentibus noctibus par priori fuit tentatio, et verbis, et osculis, et par etiam in muliere constantia. Hæc pertæsa talem ac tantam molestiam, ad Confessarii consultationem, et aliorum gravium virorum, per Exorcistas peritos fecit se exorcizare ad sciendum num esset obsessa ; et cum invenissent a nullo malo spiritu possideri, benedixerunt domui, cubiculo, lecto, et præceptum Incubo fecerunt, ne auderet molestiam amplius mulieri inferre. Sed omnia incassum : siquidem tentationem inceptam prosequebatur, ac si præ amore langueret, ploratus et ejulatus emittebat ad mulierem demulcendam, quæ tamen gratia Die adjuta semper viriliter restitit. Renovavit Incubus tentationem, ipsi apparens interdiu in forma pusionis, seu parvi homunculi pulcherrimi, cæsariem havens rutilam et crispam, barbamque fulvam ac splendentem velut aurum, glaucosque oculos, ut flos lini, incedebatque indutus habitu Hispanico. Apparebat autem illi quamvis cum ea alii morarentur ; et questus, prout faciunt amantes, exercens, et jactando basia, solitasque preces repetendo tentabat mulierem, ut ad illius amplexus admitteretur. Videbatque, et audiebat who confirmed her in her faith, exhorted her to maintain her energetic resistance and to provide herself with some holy relics. On the ensuing nights, like temptation with the same language and kisses, like constancy also on the part of the woman. Weary however of such painful and persistent molestation, taking the advice of her Confessor and other grave men, she had herself exorcised by experienced Exorcists, in order to ascertain whether perchance she was not possessed. Having found in her no trace of the evil Spirit, they blessed the house, the bed-room, the bed, and enjoined on the Incubus to discontinue his molestations. All to no purpose : he kept on worse than ever, pretending to be love-sick, weeping and moaning in order to melt the heart of the lady, who however, by the grace of God, remained unconquered. The Incubus then went another way to work : he appeared in the shape of a lad or little man of great beauty, with golden locks, a flaxen beard that shone like gold, sea-green eyes calling to mind the flax-flower, and arrayed in a fancy Spanish dress. Besides he appeared to her even when in company, whimpering, after the fashion of lovers, kissing his hand to her, and endeavouring by illa sola præsentem ac loquentem, minime autem cæteri adstantes. Perseverabat in illa constantia mulier, donec contra eam iratus Incubus, post aliquos menses blanditiarum novum persecutionis genus adortus est. Primo abstulit ab ea crucem argenteam plenam Reliquiis Sanctorum, et ceram benedictam, sive Agnum papalem B. Pontificis Pii V, quæ secum semper portabat ; mox etiam annulos et alia jocalia aurea et argentea ipsius, intactis seris sub quibus custodiebantur , in arca suffuratus est. Exinde c pit illam acriter percutere, et apparebant post verbera contusiones, et livores in facie, brachiis, aliisque corporis partibus, quæ per diem unum vel alterum perdurabant, mox in momento disparebant contra ordinem contusionis naturlais, quæ sensim paulatimque decrescit. Aliquoties ipsius infantulam lactentem cunis eripiebat, et illam, nunc super tecta in limine præcipitii locabat, nunc occultabat, nihil tamen mali in illa apparuit. Aliquoties totam domus supellectilem evertebat ; aliquoties ollas, paropsides, et alia vasa testea minutalim frangebat, subinde fracta restituebat integra. Semel dum ipsa cum viro cubaret, apparens Incubus in forma solita enixe every means to obtain her embraces. She alone saw and heard him : for every body else, he was not to be seen. The good lady kept persevering in her admirable constancy till, at last, after some months of courting, the Incubus, incensed at her disdain, had recourse to a new kind of persecution. First, he took away from her a silver cross filled with holy relics, and a holy wax or papal lamb of the blessed Pontiff Pius V, which she always carried on her person ; then, leaving the locks untouched, he purloined her rings and other gold and silver jewelry from the casket wherein they were put away. Next, he began to strike her cruelly, and after each beating bruises and marks were to be seen on her face, her arms or other parts of her body, which lasted a day or two, then suddenly disappeared, the reverse of natural bruises which decrease slowly and by degrees. Sometimes, while she was nursing her little girl, he would snatch the child away from on her breast and lay it upon the roof, on the edge of the gutter, or hide it, but without ever harming it. Sometimes he would upset all the furniture, or smash to pieces saucepans, plates and other earthenware which, in the twinkling of an eye, he restored deprecabatur ab ea concubitum, et dum ipsa de more constans resisteret, in furorem actus Incubus abscessit, et infra breve temporis spatium reversus est, secum ferens magnam copiam laminarum saxearum, quibus Genuenses in civitate sua et universa Liguria domos tegunt, et ex ipsis fabricavit murum circa lectum tantæ altitudinis, ut ejus conopeum adæquaret, unde necesse fuit scalis uti, si debuerunt de cubili surgere. Murus autem fuit absque calce, et ipso destructo, saxa in angulo seposita, quæ ibi per duos dies remanserunt visa a multis, qui ad spectaculum convenerant ; et post biduum disparuerunt. Invitaverat maritus ejus in die S. Stephani quosdam amicos viros militares ad prandium, et pro hospitum dignitate dapes paraverat ; dum de more lavantur manus ante accubitum, disparet in momento mensa parata in triclinio; disparent obsonia cuncta, olla, caldaria, patinæ, ac omnia vasa in coquina; disparent amphoræ, canthari, calices parati ad potum. Attoniti ad hoc stupent commensales, qui erant octo, inter quos Dux peditum Hispanus ad alios conversus ait : "Ne paveatis, ista est illusio, tho their former state. One night that she was lying with her husband, the Incubus, appearing in his customary shape, vehemently urged his demand which she resisted as usual. The Incubus withdrew in a rage, and shortly came back with a large load of those flag stones which the Genoese, and the inhabitants of Liguria in general, use for roofing their houses. With those stones he built around the bed a wall so high that it reached the tester, and that the couple could not leave their bed without using a ladder. This wall however was built up without lime ; when pulled down, the flags were laid by in a corner where, during two days, they were seen by many who came to look at them ; they then disappeared. On S. Stephen's day, the husband had asked some military friends to dinner, and, to do honour to his guests, had provided a substantial repast. Whilst they were, as customary, washing their hands before taking their seats, suddenly vanished the table dressed in the dining-room ; all the dishes, saucepans, kettles, plates and crockery in the kitchen vanished likewise, as well as the jugs, bottles and glasses. You may imagine the surprise, the stupor of the guests, eight in number; amongst them was a sed pro certo mensa in loco in quo erat, adhus est, et modo modo eam tactu percipiam." Hisque dictis circuibat c naculum manibus extentis, tentans mensam deprehendere, sed cum post multos circuitus incassum laborasset, et nil præter aerem tamgeret, irrisus fuit a cæteris ; cumque jam grandis esset prandii hora, pallium proprium eorum unusquisque sumpsit propriam domum petiturus. Jam erant omnes prope januam domus in procinctu eundi, associati a marito vexatæ mulieris, urbanitatis causa, cum grandem quendam strepitum in c naculo audiunt Subsistunt parumper ad cognoscendum causam strepitus, et accurrens famula nuntiat in coquina vasa nova obsoniis plena apparuisse, mensamque in c naculo jam paratam esse restitutam. Revertuntur in c naculum, et stupent mensam mappis et manutergiis insolitis, salino, et lancibus insolitis argenteis, salsamentis, ac obsoniis, quæ domi parata non fuerant, instructam. A latere magna erecta erat credentia, supra quam optimo ordine stabant calices crystallinis, argentini et aurei, cum variis amphoris, lagenis, cantharis plenis vinis exteris, puta Cretensi, Campano, Canariensi, Rhenano, etc. In coquina pariter in ollis, et vasis itidem in ea domo nunquam visis, varia obsonia. Dubitarunt

Spanish Captain of infantry, who, addressing the company, said to them : "Do not be frightened, it is but a trick : the table is certainly still where it stood, and I shall soon find it by feeling for it". Having thus spoken, he paced round the room with outstretched arms, endeavouring to lay hold of the table; but when, after many circuitous perambulations, it was apparent that he laboured in vain and grasped at nought but thin air, he was laughed at by his friends ; and it being already high time for having dinner, each guest took up his cloak and set about to return home. They had already reached the street-door with the husband, who, out of politeness, was attending them, when they heard a great noise in the dining-room : they stood to ascertain the cause thereof, and presently the servant came up to announce that the kitchen was stocked with new vessels filled with food, and that the table was standing again in its former place. Having gone back to the dining-room, they were stupefied to see the table was laid, with cloths, napkins, salt-cellars, and trays that did not belong to the house, and with food which had not been cooked there. On a large sideboard all were arrayed in perfect order crystal, silver and gold chalices, with all prius nonnulli ex iis eas dapes gustare, sed confirmati ab aliis accubuerunt, et exquisitissime omnia condita repererunt ; ac immediate a prandio, dum omnes pro usu illius tempores ad ignem sedent, omnia ustensilia cum reliquiis ciborum desparuere, et repertæ sunt antiquæ domus supellectiles simul cum dapibus, quæ prius paratæ fuerant ; et quod mirum est, convivæ omnes saturati sunt, ita ut nullus eorum cænam sumpserit præ prandii lautitia. Quo convincitur cibos appositos reales fuisse, et non ex præstigio repræsentatos. Interea effluxerant multi menses, ex quos cæperant hujusmodi persecutio : et mulier votum fecit B. Bernardino Feltrensi, cumus sacrum corpus veneratur in Ecclesia S. Jacobi prope murum illius urbis, incedendi per annum integrum indutam panno griseo, et chordulato, quo utuntur Fratres Minores, de quorum ordine fuit B. Bernardinus, ut per ipsius patrocinium a tanta Incubi vexatione liberaretur. Et de facto kind of amphoras, decanters and cups filled with foreign wines, from the Isle of Crete, Campania, the Canaries, the Rhine, etc. In the kitchen there was also an abundant variety of meats in saucepans and dishes that had never been seen there before. At first, some of the guests hesitated whether they should taste of that food; however, encouraged by others, they sat down, and soon partook of the meal, which was found exquisite. Immediately afterwards, as they were sitting before a seasonable fire, every thing vanished at once, the dishes and the leavings, and in their stead reappeared the cloth of the house and the victual which had been previously cooked; but, for a wonder, all the guests were satisfied, so that no one thought of supper after such a magnificent dinner. A clear proof that the substituted viands were real and nowise fictitious. This kind of persecution had been going on some months, when the lady betook herself to the blessed Bernardino of Feltri, whose body is worshiped in the church of St James, a short distance from the walls of the city. She made a vow to him that she would wear, during a whole twelve-month, a grey frock, tied round her waist with a piece of cord, and such as is worn by the Minor Brethren, the order die 28 Septembris, qui est pervigilium Dedicationis S. Michaelis Archangeli, et festum B. Bernardini, ipsa veste votiva induta est. Mane sequenti, quod est festum S. Michaelis, ibat vexata ad ecclesiam S. Michaelis, quæ ut diximus erat parochialis ipsius, circa medium mane, dum frequens populus ad illam confluebat ; et cum pervenisset ad medium plateæ ecclesiæ, omnia ipsius indumenta et ornamenta ceciderunt in terram et rapta vento statim disparuerunt, ipsa relicta nuda. Adfuerunt sorte inter alios duo equites viri longævi, qui factum videntes, dejectis ab humero propriis palliis mulieris nuditatem, ut potuerunt, velarunt, et rhedæ impositam ad propriam domum duxerunt. Vestes et jocalia quæ rapuerat Incubus, non restituit nisi post sex menses. Multa alia, et quidem stupenda operatus est contra eam Incubus, quæ tædet exscribere, et per multos annos in ea tentatione to which had belonged the blessed Bernardine ; this she vowed, in the hope of being, through his intercession, at last rid of the persecution of the Incubus. And accordingly, on the 28th of September, the vigil of the Dedication of the Archangel S. Michael, and the festival of the blessed Bernardine, she assumed the votive robe. The next morning, which was S. Michael's festival, the afflicted woman proceeded to the church of St Michael, her own parish, already mentioned ; it was about ten o'clock, a time when a crowd of people were going to mass. She had no sooner set foot on the treshold of the church, than her clothes and ornaments fell off to the ground, and disappeared in a gust of wind, leaving her stark naked. There happened fortunately to be among the crowd two cavaliers of mature age, who, seeing what had taken place, hastened to divest themselves of their cloaks with which they concealed, as well as they could, the woman's nudity, and having put her into a vehicle, accompanied her home. The clothes and trinkets taken by the Incubus were not restored by him before six months had elapsed. I might relate many other most surprising tricks which that Incubus played on her, were it not wearisome. Suffice it to say that, permansit ; tandemque Incubus videns operam in ea perdere, destitit a tam importuna et insolita vexatione. 29. In hoc casu, et similibus qui passim audiuntur et leguntur, Incubus ad nullum actum contra Religionem tentat, sed solum contra castitatem. Hinc fit quod ipsi consentiens non peccat irreligiositate, sed incontinentia. 30. In confesso autem est apud Theologos et Philosophos, quod ex commixtione hominis cum Dæmone aliquoties nascuntur homines, et tali modo nasciturum esse Antichristum opinantur nonnulli Doctores : Bellarm.lib.I, de Rom. Pont., cap.I2; Suarez, tom. 2., disp. 54, sec. I.; Maluend., de Antichr., l. 2., c. 8. Immo observant, quod, qui gignuntur ab hujusmodi Incubis, naturali causa etiam evenit, ut nascantur grandes, robustissimi, ferocissimi, superbissimi,ac nequissimi, ut scripsit Maluenda, loc. Cit., § Ad illud ; et hujus rationem recitat ex Vallesio Archia. Reggio. Sac. Philosoph., c. 8., dicente quod Incubi summittant in uteros non qualecumque, neque quantumcumque semen, sed plurimum, crassissimum, calidissimum, spiritibus affluens for a number of years he persevered in his temptation of her, but that finding at last that he was losing his pains, he desisted from his vexatious importunities. 29. In the above case, as well as in others that may be heard or read of occasionally, the Incubus attempts no act against Religion ; he merely assails chastity. In consequence, consent is not a sin through ungodliness, but through incontinence. 30. Now, it is undoubted by Theologians and philosophers that carnal intercourse between mankind and the Demon sometimes gives birth to human beings ; that is how is to be born the Antichrist, according to some Doctors, such as Bellarmin, Suarez, Maluenda, etc. They further observe that, from a natural cause, the children thus begotten by Incubi are tall, very hardy and bold, very proud and wicked. Thus writes Maluenda ; as for the cause, he gives it from Vallesius, Archphysician in Reggio : "What Incubi introduce in uteros, is not qualecumque neque quantumcumque semen, but abundant, very thick, very warm, rich in spirits and free from serosity. This moreover is an easy thing for them, since they have but to choose et seri expers. Id vero est eis facile conquirere, deligendo homines calidos, robustos, et abondantes multo semine, quibus succumbant, deinde et mulieres tales, quibus incumbant, atque utrisque voluptatem solito majorem afferendo, tanto enim abundantius emittitur semen, quanto cum majori voluptate excernitur. Hæc Vallesius. Confirmat vero Maluenda supradicta, probando, ex variis et classicis Auctoribus, ex hujusmodi concubitu natos : Romulum ac Remum, Liv. decad. I ; Plutarch., in Vit. Romul. et Parallel. ; Servium Tullium, sextum regem Romanorum, Dionys. Halicar., lib. 4, Plin., lib. 36., c. 27 ; Platonem Philosophum, Laer. l., 9. de Vit. Philos.; D. Hyeron., l. I. Controvers. Jovinian.; Alexandrum Magnum, Plutarch., in Vit. Alex. M.; Quint. Curt., l. 4, de Gest. Alex. M.; Seleucum, regem Syriæ, Just., Hist., l. 15 ; Appian., in Syriac. ; Scipionem Africanum Majorem, Liv., decad. 3, lib. 6 ; Cæsarem Augustum Imperatorem, Sueton., in Octa., c. 94 ; Aristomenem Messenium, strenuissimum ducem Græcorum , Strabo, de Sit Orb., lib. 8 ; Pausan., de Rebus Græcor., lib. 3 ; et Merlinum, seu Melchinum Anglicum ex Incubo et Filia Caroli Magni Moniali, Hauller, volum. 2, Generat. 7, quod etiam de Martino Luthero,perditissimo ardent, robust men, et abundantes multo semine, quibus succumbant, and then women of a like constitution, quibus incumbant, taking care that both shall enjoy voluptatem solito majorem, tanto enim abundantius emittitur semen, quanto cum majori voluptate excernitur." Those are the words of Vallesius, confirmed by Maluenda who shows, from the testimony of various Authors, mostly classical, that such associations gave birth to : Romulus and Remus, according to Livy and Plutarch; Servius-Tullius, the sixth king of Rome, according to Dyonisius of Halicarnassus and Pliny the Elder; Plato the Philosopher, according to Diogenes Laertius and Saint Hieronymus; Alexander the Great, according to Plutarch and Quintus-Curtius; Seleucus, king of Syria, according to Justinus and Appianus; Scipio Africanus the Elder, according to Livy ; the emperor Cæsar Augustus, according to Suetonius; Aristomenes the Messenian, an illustrious Greek commander, according to Strabo and Pausanias ; as also Merlin or Melchin the Englishman, born from an Incubus and a nun, the daughter of Charlemagne ; and, lastly, as shown by the writings of Cochlæus quoted by Maluenda, that damned Heresiarch ycleped Martin Luther.

Heresiarcha scribit Cohlæus apud Maluendam, de Antich., lib. 2, c. 6, Cæterum. 3I. Salva tament tot, et tantorum Doctorum, qui in ea opinione conveniunt, reverentia, non video, quomodo ipsorum setentia possit subsistere; tum quia, ut optime opinatur Pererius, tom. 2, in Genes., cap. 6, disp. 5, tota vis et efficacia humani seminis consistit in spiritibus, qui difflantur, et evanescunt statim ac sunt extra genitalia vasa, a quibus foventur et conservantur, ut scribunt Medici. Nequit proinde Dæmon semen acceptum conservare, ita ut aptum sit generationi, quia vas, quodcumque sit illud, in quo semen conservare tentaret, oporteret quod caleret calore assimetro a nativo organorum hamanæ generationis ; similarem enim a nullo alio præterquam ab organis ipsis habere potest generatio. Tum quia generatio actus vitalis est, per quem homo generans de propria substantia semen defert per organa naturalia ad locum generationi congruentem. In casu autem delatio seminis non potest esse actus vitalis hominis generantis, quia ab eo non infertur in matricem ; proinde nec dici potest, quod homo

31. However, with due deference to so many and such learned Doctors, I hardly see how their opinion can bear examination. For, as Pererius truly observes in his Commentary on the Genesis, chapt. 6, the whole strength and efficiency of the human sperm reside in the spirits which evaporate and vanish as soon as issued from the genital vessels wherein they were warmly stored: all medical men agree on that point. It is consequently not possible that the Demon should preserve in a fit state for generation the sperm he has received ; for it were necessary that whatever vessel he endeavoured to keep it in should be equally warm with the human genital organs, the warmth of which is nowhere to be met with but in those organs themselves. Now, in a vessel where that warmth is not intrinsical but extraneous, the spirits get altered, and no generation can take place. There is this other objection, that generation is a vital act by which man, begetting from his own substance, carries the sperm through natural organs to the spot which is appropriate to generation. On the contrary, in this particular case, the introduction of sperm cannot be a vital act of the man who begets, since it is not carried into the womb by his agency ; and, for

eujus est semen, generat f tum, qui ex eo nascitur. Neque Incubus ipsius pater dici potest ; quia de ipsius substantia semen non est. Hinc fiet, quod nascetur homo, cujus nemo pater sit, quod est congruum. Tum quia in patre naturaliter generante duplex causalitas concurrit, nempe materialis, quia semen, quod materia generationis, ministrat, et efficiens, quia agens principale est in generatione, ut communiter statuunt Philosophi. In casu autem nostro homo ministrando solum semen, puram materiam exhiberet absque ulla actione in ordine ad generationem ; proinde non posset dici pater filii qui nasceretur : et hoc est contra id, quod homo genitus ab Incubo non est illius filius, sed est filius ejus viri, a quo Incubus semen sumpsit. 32. Præterea omni probabilitate, caret quod scribit Vallesius, et ex eo recitavimus the same cause, it cannot be said that the man, whose sperm it was, has begotten the fetus which proceeds from it. Nor can the Incubus be deemed its father, since the sperm does not issue from his own substance. Consequentially, a child would be born without a father, which is absurd. Third objection : when the father begets in the course of nature, there is a concurrence of two casualties : the one, material, for he provides the sperm which is the matter of generation ; the other, efficient, for he is the principal agent of generation, as Philosophers agree in declaring. But, in this case, the man who only provided the sperm would contribute but a mere material, without any action tending to generation ; he could therefore not be regarded as the father of the child begotten under those circumstances ; and this is opposed to the notion that the child begotten by an Incubus is not his son, but the son of the man whose sperm the Incubus has taken. 32. Besides, there is not a shadow of probability in what was written by Vallesius and quoted from him by us (Vide supra n 30); and I wonder that any thing so extravagant should have fallen from supra n 30 ; mirorque a doctissimi viri calamo talia excidisse. Notissimum enim est apud Physicos, quod magnitudo fœtus non est a quantitate molis, sed est a quantitate virtutis, hoc est spirituum in semine : ab ea enim tota generationis ratio dependet, ut optime testatur Michael Ettmullerus, Instit. Medic. Physiolog., car. 22, thes. I, fol. M., 39, scribens : Tota generationis ratio dependet a spiritu genitali sub crassioris materiæ involucro excreto ; ista materia seminis crassa nullo modo, vel in utero subsistente, vel seu materia fœtum constituente : sed solus spiritus genitalis maris unitus cum spiritu genitali mulieris in poros uteri, seu quod rarius fit, in tubos uteri se insinuat, indeque uterum fecundum reddit. Quid ergo facere potest magna quantitas seminis ad fœtus magnitudinem? Præterea nec semper verum est, quod tales geniti ab Incubis magnitudien molis corporeæ insignes sint : Alexander enim Magnus, qui ut diximus, natus taliter scribitur, statura pusillus erat ; unde carmen, Magnus Alexander corpore parvus erat. Item quamvis taliter concepti supra cæteros homines excellant, non tamen hoc semper est in vitiis, sed aliquando in virtutibus the pen of such a learned man. Medical men are well aware that the size of the fetus depends, not indeed on the quantity of matter, but on the quantity of virtue, that is to say of spirits held by the sperm ; there lies the whole secret of generation, as is well observed by Michael Ettmuller, Institut. Medic. Physiology. : "Generation", says he, "entirely depends upon the genital spirit contained within an envelope of thicker matter ; that spermatic matter does not remain in the uterus, and has no share in the formation of the fetus ; it is but the genital spirit of the male, combined with the genital spirit of the female, that permeates the pores, or, less frequently, the tubes of the uterus, which it fecundates by that means." Of what moment can therefore the quantity of sperm be for the size of the fetus? Besides, it is not always a fact that men thus begotten by Incubi are remarkable for the huge proportions of their body: Alexander the Great, for instance, who is said to have been thus born, as we have mentioned, was very short ; as the poet said of him : Magnus Alexander corpore parvus erat. Besides, although it is generally a fact that those who are thus begotten excel etiam in moralibus, ut patet in Scipione Africano, Cæsare Augusto, et Platone Philosopho, de quibus Livius, Suetonius et Laertius respective scribunt, quod optimi in moribus fuere ; ut proinde arguere possimus, quod si alii eodem modo geniti pessimi fuere, hoc non fuerit ex hoc, quod fuerint ab Incubo geniti, sed quia tales exproprio arbitrio exstitere. Pariter ex textu Sacæ Scripturæ, Gen., c. 6, v. 4, habemus quod gigantes nati sunt ex concubitu filiorum Dei cum filiabus hominum, et hoc ad litteram sacri textus. Gigantes autem homines erant statura magna, ut eos vocat Baruch, c. 3, v. 26, et excedente communem hominum proceritatem. Monstruosa statura, robore, latrociniis, et tyrannide insignes : unde Gigantes per sua scelera fuerunt maxima, et potissima causa Diluvii, ait Cornelius a Lapid. in Gen., c. 6, v. 4, § Burgensis. Non quadrat autem quorumdam expositio, quod nomine filiorum Dei veniant filii Seth, et vocabulo filiarum hominum filiæ Cain, eo quod illi erant pietati, Religioni, et cæteris virtutibus addicti, descendentes autem a other men, yet such superiority is not always shown by their vices, but sometimes by their virtues and even their morals ; Scipio Africanus, for instance, Cæser Augustus and Plato the Philosopher, as is recorded of each of them respectively by Live, Suetonius and Diogenes Laertius, had excellent morals. Whence may be inferred that, if other individuals begotten in the same way have been downright villains, it was not owing to their being born of an Incubus, but to their having, of their own free will, chosen to be such. We also read in the Testament, Genesis, chap. 6, verse 4, that giants were born when the sons of God came in unto the daughters of men : that is the very letter of the sacred text. Now, those giants were men of great stature, says Baruch,chap. 3, verse 26, and far superior to other men. Not only were they distinguished by their huge size, but also by their physical power, their plundering habits and their tyranny. Through their criminal excesses the Giants were the primary and principal cause of the Flood, according to Cornelius a Lapide, in his Commentary on Genesis. Some contend that by Sons of God are meant the sons of Seth, and by Daughters

Cain vice versa : nam salva opinantium, Chrysost., Cyrill.,Theodor. Rupert. Ab. et Hilar. in Psalm. 132, apud Cornel., a Lap., c. 6 ; G., v. 2, § Verum dies, reverentia, talis expositio non cohæret sensui patenti litteræ ; ait enim Scriptura, quod ex conjunctione talium nati sunt homines monstruosæ proceritatis corporeæ : ante illam ergo tales gigantes non extiterunt : quod si ex ea orti sunt, hoc non potuit esse ex eo, quod filii Seth coivissent cum filiabus Cain, quia illi erant staturæ ordinariæ, prout etiam filiæ Cain, unde oriri ex his naturaliter non potuerunt nisi filii statur ordinariæ : si ergo monstruosa statura filii nati sunt ex tali conjunctione, hoc fuit, quia non fuerunt prognati ex ordinaria conjunctione viri cum muliere, sed ex Incubis dæmonibus qui ratione naturæ ipsorum optime possunt vocari filii Dei, et in hac sententia sunt Philosophi Platonici, et Franciscus Georgius Venetus, tom. I, problem. 74 : nec dissentiunt ab eadem Joseph Hebræus, Philo Judæus, S. Justinus Martyr, Clemens Alexandrinus, et Tertullianus, Joseph. Hebræus, Antiq., l. I.; Philo, l. de Giant.; S. Justinus M., Apolog. I.; Clemens Alex., lib. 3; Tertull., lib. de Habit. Mul., apud Cornel., loc. cit.; Hugo de S. Victor., Annot. in Gen., c. 6, of men the daughters of Cain, because the former practiced piety, religion and every other virtue, whilst the descendants of Cain were quite the reverse; but, with all due deference to Chrysostom, Cyrillus, Hilarius and others who are of that opinion, it must be conceded that it clashes with the obvious meaning of the text.Scripture says, in fact, that of the conjunction of the above mentioned were born men of huge bodily size : consequently, those giants were not previously in existence, and if their birth was the result of that conjunction, it cannot be ascribed to the intercourse of the sons of Seth with the daughters of Cain, who being themselves of ordinary stature, could but procreate children of ordinary stature. Therefore, if the intercourse in question gave birth to beings of huge stature, the reason is that it was not the common connection between man and woman, but the performance of Incubi Demons who, from their nature, may very well be styled sons of God. Such is the opinion of the Platonist Philosophers and of Francis Georges the Venetian; nor is it discrepant from that of Josephus the Historian, Philo the Jew, S. Justinus the Martyr, Clement of Alexandria, and Tertullian, who look upon Incubi as corporeal qui opinantur illos fuisse Angelos quosnam corporeos qui in luxuriam cum mulieribus delapsi sunt : ut enim infra ostendemus, istæ duæ sententiæ in unam et eamdem conveniunt. 33. Si ergo Incubi tales, ut fert communis sententia, Gigantes genuerunt, accepto semine ab homine, juxta id, quod supra dictum est, non potuerunt ex illo semine nasci nisi homines ejusdem staturæ plus minusve, cum eo a quo semen acceptum est : nec enim facit ad altiorem corporis staturam major seminis quantitas, ita ut attracta insolite a Dæmone, dum Succubus fit homini, augeat ultra illius staturam enormiter corpus ab eo geniti ; quia, ut supra diximus, hoc resident in spiritu, et non in mole seminis : ut proinde necesse sit concludere, quob ab alio semine, quam humano, hujusmodi gigantes nati sint, et proinde Dæmon Incubus non humano, sed alio semine utatur ad generationem. Quid igitur dicendum?

Angels who have allowed themselves to fall into the sin of lewdness with women. Indeed, as shall be shown hereafter, though seemingly distinct, those two opinions are but one and the same.
33. If therefore these Incubi, in conformity with general belief, have begotten Giants by means of sperm taken from man, it is impossible, as aforesaid, that of that sperm should have been born any but men of approximately the same size as he from whom it came; for it would be in vain for the Demon, when acting the part of a Succubus, to draw from man an unwonted quantity of prolific liquor in order to procreate therefrom children of higher stature; quantity has nothing to do here, since all depends, as we have said, upon the vitality of that liquor, not its quantity. We are therefore bound to infer that Giants are born of another sperm than man's, and that, consequently, the Incubus Demon, for the purpose of generation, uses a sperm which is not man's. But then, what is to be said?

34. Quantum ad hoc, sub correctione Santæ Matris Ecclesiæ, et mere opinative dico, Incubum Dæmonem, dum mulieribus commiscetur, ex proprio ipsius semine hominem generare. 35. Paradoxa in fide, et parum sana nonnullis videbitur hæc opinio ; sed lectorem meum deprecor, ut judicium non præcipitet de ea : ut enim incivile est nondum tota lege perspecta judicare, ut Celsus, lib. 24. ff. de legib. et S. C., ait, ita neque dammanda est opinio, nisi prius examinatis, ac solutis argumentis, quibus innititur. Ad probandam igitur supradatam conclusionem, nonnulla sunt necessario præmittenda. 36. Præmittendum primo de fide est, quod dentur Creaturæ pure spirituales nullo modo de materia corporea participantes, prout habetur ex Concilio Lateranensi, sub Innocentio Tertio, c. Firm. de Sum. Trin. et Fid. Cath. Conc. Eph. in Epist. Cyrill. ad Reggia, et alibi. Hujusmodi autem sunt Angeli beati, et Dæmones damnati ad ignem perpetuum. Quamvis vero nonnulli Doctores, Bann.

34. Subject to correction by our Holy Mother Church, and as a mere expression of opinion, I say that the Incubus Demon, when having intercourse with women, bigets the human fetus from his own sperm. 35. To many that proposition will seem heterodox and hardly sensible ; but I beg of my reader not to condemn it precipitately ; for if, as Celsus says, it is improper to deliver judgment without having thoroughly inquired into the law, no less unfair is the rejection of an opinion, before the arguments upon which it rests have been weighed and confuted. I have therefore to prove the above conclusion, and must necessarily premise with some statements. 36. Firstly, I premise, as an article of belief, that there are purely spiritual creatures, not in any way partaking of corporeal matter, as was ruled by the Council of Lateran, under the pontificate of Innocent III. Such are the blessed Angels, and the Demons condemned to ever-lasting fire. Some Doctors, it is true, have professed, subsequently even to this Council, that the spirituality of Angels and Demons

par. I. q. 5. ar. I. Can. de Loc. Theol. l. 5. c. 5. Sixt. seu Bibliot. San. l. 5. annot. 8., Mirand. Sum. Council. v . Angelus, Molina, p. I. q. 50., a. I., Carranz., Annot. ad Synod. 7., etiam post Concilium illud docuerint spiritualitatem Angelorum et Dæmonum non esse de fide, ita ut nonnulli alii, Bonav. in lib. 2. sent. dist. 3. q. I., Scot. de Anim. q. I5., Cajet. in Gen. c. 4., Franc. Geor. Problem. l. 2. c. 57., August. Hyph., de Dæmon., l. 3. c. 3., scripserint illos esse corporeos, et proinde Angelos Dæmonosque corpore et spiritu constare non esse propositionem hæreticam, neque erroneam, probet Bonaventura Baro, Scot. Defens. tom. 9. apolog. 2., act. I., p. 7. : tamen quia Concilium ipsum statuit de fide tenendum, Deum esse Creatorem omnium visibilium et invisibilium, spiritualium et corporalium, qui utramque de nihilo condidit creaturam spiritualem et corporalem Angelicam, videlicet ut mundanam : ideo dico de fide esse quasdam creaturas dari mere spirituales, et tales esse Angelos, non quidem omnes, sed quosdam. 37. Inaudita forsan erit sententia hæc, sed non destituta erit probabilitate. Si enim a Theologis tanta inter Angelos diversitas is not an article of belief; others even have asserted that they are corporeal, whence Bonaventure Baron has drawn the conclusion that it is neither heretical nor erroneous to ascribe to Angels and Demons a twofold substance, corporeal and spiritual. Yet, the Council having formally declared it to be an article of belief that God is the maker of all things visible and invisible, spiritual and corporeal, who has raised from nothing every creature spiritual or corporeal, Angelic or terrestrial, I contend it is an article of belief that there are certain merely spiritual creatures, and that such are Angels ; not all of them, but a certain number. 37. It may seem strange, yet it must be admitted not to be unlikely. If, in fact, Theologians concur in establishing specifica, et proinde essentialis statuitur, ut in via D. Thomæ, p. p. 50, ar. 4, plures Angeli nequeant esse in eadem specie, sed quilibet Angelus propriam speciem costituat, profecto nulla invenitur repugnantia, quod Angelorum nonnulli sint purissimi spiritus, et proinde excellentisimæ naturæ, alii autem corporei, et minus excellentes, et eorum differentia petatur per corporeum et incorporeum. Accedit quod hac sententia facile solvitur alias insolubilis contradictio inter duo Concilia cumeica, nempe Septimam Synodum generalem, et dictum Concilium Lateranense : siquidem in illa Synodo, quæ est secunda Nicæna, actione quinta, productus est liber Joannis Thessalonicensis scriptus contra quemdam Philosphum gentilem, in quo ita habetur : De Angelis et Archangelis, atque eorum Potestatibus, quibus nostras Animas adjungo ipsa Catholica Ecclesia sic sentit, esse quidem intelligibiles, sed non omnino corporis expertes, et insensibiles, ut vos Gentiles dicitis, verum tenui corpore præditos, et aereo, sive igneo, sicut scriptum est : qui facit Angelos suos spiritus, et ministros suos ignem urentem. Et infra : Quamquam autem non sint ut nos, corporei, utpote ex quatuor elementis, nemo tamen vel amongst Angels a specific, and therefore essential, diversity so considerable that, according to St. Thomas, there are not two Angels of the same species, but that each of them is a species by himself, why should not certain Angels be most pure spirits, of a consequently very superior nature, and others corporeal, therefore of a less perfect nature, differing thus from each other in their corporeal or incorporeal substance? This doctrine has the advantage of solving the otherwise insoluble contradiction between two cumenical Councils, namely the Seventh General Synod and the above-mentioned Council of Lateran. For, during the fifth sitting of that Synod, the second of Nice, a book was introduced written by John of Thessalonica against a pagan Philosopher, wherein occur the following propositions : "Respecting Angels, Archangels and their Powers, to which I adjoin our own Souls, the Catholic Church is really of opinion that they are intelligences, but not entirely bodyless and senseless, as you Gentiles aver ; she on the contrary ascribes to them a subtile body, aerial or igneous, according to what is written : He makes the spirits His Angels, and the burning fire His Minister". And further on : "Although not corporeal in the

Angelos, vel Dæmones, vel Animas dixerit incorporeas : multoties enim in proprio corpore visi sunt ab illis, quibus Donimus oculos aperuit. Et cum omnia lecta fuissent coram Patribus synodaliter congregatis, Tharasius, Patriarcha Constantinopolitanus, poposcit adprobationem Sanctæ Synodi his verbis : Ostendit Pater, quod Angelos pingi oporteat, quonim circumscribi possunt, et ut homines apparuerunt. Synodus autem uno ore respondit : Etiam, Domine. 38. Hanc autem Conciliarem adprobationem de materia ad longum pertractata a D. Joanne in libro coram Patribus lecto, statuere articulum fidei circa corporeitatem Angelorum, perspicuum est : unde ad tollendam contradictionem hujus, cum allata definitione Concilii Lateranensis, multum desudant Theologi. Unus enim, Suarez, de Angelis, ait quod Patres non contradixerunt tali asserto de corporeitate Angelorum, quia non de illa re agebatur. Alius, Bann., in p. p. q. 10, ait, quod Synodus adprobavit conclusionem, nempe Angelos pingi posse, non tamen adprobavit same way as ourselves, made of the four elements, yet it is impossible to say that Angels, Demons and Souls are incorporeal ; for they have been seen many a time, invested with their own body, by those whose eyes the Lord had opened". And after that book had been read through before all the Fathers in Council assembled, Tharasius, the Patriarch of Constantinople, submitted it to the approval of the Council, with these words: "The Father showeth that Angels should be pictured, since their form can be defined, and they have been seen in the shape of men". Without a dissentient, the Synod answered: "Yes, my Lord". 38. That this approbation by a Council of the doctrine set forth at length in the book of John establishes an article of belief with regard to the corporeity of Angels, there is not a shadow of doubt : so Theologians toil and moil in order to remove the contradiction apparent between that decision and the definition, above quoted, by the Council of Lateran. One of them, Suarez, says that if the Fathers did not disprove such an assertion of the corporeity of Angels, it is because that was not the question. Another contends that the Synod did approve the conclusion, namely rationem, quia corporei sunt. Alius, Molin., in p. p., q. 50. a. I, ait quod definitiones Conciliares in illa Synodo factoæ sunt solum actione septima, proinde ea quæ habentur in actionibus præcedentibus no esse definitiones de fide. Alii, Joverc. et Mirand., Sum. Conc., scribunt nec Nicænum, nec Lateranense Concilium intendisse definere de fide quætionem; et Nicænum quidem locutum fuisse juxta opinionem Platonicorum, quæ ponit Angelos corporeos, et tunc prævalebat ; Lateranense autem locutum esse juxta mentem Aristotelis, qui, l. 12. Metaphys., tex. 49, ponit intelligentias incorporeas, quæ sententia contra Platonicos apud plerosque Doctores invaluit expost. 39. Sed quam frigidæ sint istæ responsiones nemo non videt, ac eas minime satisfacere oppositioni palmariter demonstrat Bonaventura Baro, Scot. Defens., tom. 9, apolog. 2, actio I, § 2 per totum. Proinde ad tollendam contradictionem Conciliorum dicendum est, Nicæum locutum esse de una, Lateranense autem de alia specie Angelorum, et illan quidem corpoream, hanc vero penitus incorpoream ;

that Angels might be pictured, but not the motive given, their corporeity. A third, Molina, observes that the definitions issued in Council by the Synod were thus issued only at the seventh sitting, whence he argues that those of the previous sittings are not definitions of belief. Others, lastly, write that neither the Council of Nicea nor that of Lateran intended defining a question of belief, the Council of Nicea having spoken according to the opinion of the Platonists, which describes Angels as corporeal beings and was then prevailing, whilst that of Lateran went with Aristoteles, who, in his 12th. book of Metaphysics, lays down the existence of incorporeal intelligences, a doctrine which has since carried the day with most Doctors over the Platonists. 39. But any one can discern the invalidity of those answers, and Bonaventure Baro (Scot. Defens., tome 9) proves to evidence that they do not bear. In consequence, in order to agree the two Councils, we must say that the Council of Nicea meant one species of Angels, and that of Lateran another : the former, corporeal, the latter on the contrary absolutely incorporeal; and thus are reconciled et sic conciliantur aliter irrreconciliabilia Concilia. 40. Præmittendum 2 , nomen Angeli esse nomen officii, non naturæ, ut concorditer scribunt S. S.Patres : Ambros: in c. I epist. ad Hebr., Hilaris, l. 5 de Trin., Augustinus, lib. 15 de Civit. Dei c. 23, Gregorius, Hom. 34 in Evang., Isidorus, l. de Sum. Bonit., c. 12 ; unde præclare ait D. Ambrosius : Angelus non ex eo quod est spiritus, ex eo quod agit, Angelus, quia Angelus Græce, Latine Nuntius dicitur; sequitur igitur ex hoc, quod illi, qui ad aliquod ministerium a. Deo mittuntur, sive spiritus sint, sive homines, Angeli vocari possunt; et de facto ita vocantur in Scripturis Sacris : nam de Sacerdotibus, Concionatoribus ac Doctoribus, qui tanquam Nuntii Dei explicant hominibus divinam voluntatem, dicitur, Malach. c. 2. v. 7 : Labia Sacerdotis custodient scientiam, et legem requirent ex ore ejus, quia Angelus Domini exercituum est. D. Joannes Baptista ab eodem Propheta, c. 3 v. I, vocatur Angelus, dum ait : Ecce ego mitto Angelum meam et præparabit viam ante faciem meam. Et hanc prophetiam esse ad litteram de S. Joanne Baptista testatur Christus Dominus two otherwise irreconcilable Councils. 40. Secondly, I premise that the word Angel applies, not indeed to the kind, but to the office : the Holy Fathers are agreed thereupon (St. Ambrose, on the Epistle to the Hebrews; St. Austin, City of God; St. Gregory, Homily 34 on Scripture; St. Isidorus, Supreme Goodness). An Angel, very truly says St. Ambrose, is thus styled, not because he is a spirit, but on account of his office : [Greek omitted] in Greek, Nuntius in Latin, that is to say Messenger; it follows that whoever is entrusted by God with a mission, be he spirit or man, may be called an Angel, and is thus called in the Holy Scriptures, where the following words are applied to Priests, Preachers and Doctors, who, as Messengers of God, explain to men the divine will (Malachi, chapt. 2, v. 7). "The priest's lips should keep knowledge, and they should seek the law at his mouth, for he is the Angel of the Lord of Hosts." The same prophet, chapt. 3, v. 1, bestows the name of Angel on St. John the Baptist, when saying: "Behold, I will send my Angel and he shall prepare the way before me." That this prophecy literally applies to St. John the Baptist is in Evangelio Matthæi, II, v. 10. Immo et ipse Deus, quia fuit missus a Patre in mundum ad evangelizandum legem gratiæ, vocatur Angelus. Ita in prophetia Isaiæ, c. 9 v. 6, juxta versionem Septuaginta : Vocabitur nomen ejus magni consilii Angelus, et clarius in Malachiæ c. 3 v. I : Veniet ad templum sanctum suum Dominator quem vos quæritis, et Angelus testamenti quem vos vultis. Quæ prophetia ad litteram est de Christo Domino. Sequitur igitur nullum absurdum sequi ex hoc, quod dicimus Angelos quosdam esse corporeos, nam et homines, qui corpore constant, Angeli vocabulo efferuntur. 41. Præmittendum 3 , nondum rerum naturalium, quæ sunt in mundo, satis perspectam esse existentiam, aut naturam, ut proinde aliquid negandum sit ex eo, quod de illo nunquam alias dictum, aut scriptum fuerit. Patet enim tractu temporis detectas esse novas terras, quas Antiqui nostri ignorarunt, novaque animalia, herbas, plantas, fructus, semina nunquam alias visa ; et si pervia esset Terra Australis incognita, cujus indagatio, et lustratio testified by our Lord Jesus-Christ, in the Gospel, according to St. Matthew, chapt. II, v. 10. Still more : God himself is called an Angel, because he has been sent by His Father to herald the law of mercy. To witness, the prophecy of Isaiah, chapt. 9, v. 6, according to Septuagint : "He shall be called an Angel of Wonderful Counsel." And more plainly still in Malachi, chapt. 3, v. I : "The Lord whom ye seek shall suddenly come to his temple, even the Angel of the covenant whom ye delight in", a prophecy which literally applies to our Lord Jesus-Christ. There is consequently nothing absurd in the contention that some Angels are corporeal, since men, who assuredly have a body, are called Angels. 41. Thirdly, I premise that neither the existence nor the nature of the natural things in this world has been sufficiently investigated to allow of denying a fact, merely because it has never been previously spoken of or written about. In the course of time have not new lands been discovered which the Ancients knew not of? New animals, herbs, plants, fruits and seeds, never seen elsewhere? And if that mysterious Austral land came at last to be explored, a multis hucusque incassum tentata est, adhuc nova nobis alia panderentur. Patet adhuc, quod per inventionem microscopii, et alias machinas, et organa Philosophiæ experimentalis modernæ, sicut etiam per exactiorem indaginem Anatomistarum, multarum rerum naturalium existentiam, vires, naturamque tum innotuisse, tum dietim innotescere, quæ præcedentes Philosophi ignorarunt, ut patet in auro fulminante, phosphoro, et centum aliis chymicis experimentis, circulatione sanguinis, venis lacteis, vasis lymphaticis, et aliis hujusmondi quæ nuper Anatomistæ adinvenerunt. Proinde ineptum erit aliquod exsibillare ex hoc quod de eo nullus Antiquorum scripserit, attento maxime Logicorum axiomate, quod locus ab auctoritate negativa non tenet. 42. Præmittendum 4 , quod in Sacra Scriptura, et Ecclesiasticis traditionibus non traditur nisi id, quod ad animæ salutem necessarium est, quoad credendum, sperandum et amandum; unde inferre non licet ex eo, quod nec ex Scriptura, nec ex traditione aliquod habetur, proinde negandum as has been to this day vainly tried by so many travellers, what unforeseen disclosures would be the result! Through the invention of the microscope and other instruments used by modern experimental Philosophy, combined with the more exact methods of investigation of Anatomists, have there not been, and are there not, every day, brought to light the existence, qualities and characteristics of a number of natural things unknown to ancient Philosophers, such as fulminating gold, phosphorus, and a hundred other chemical compounds, the circulation of the blood, the lacteal vessels, the lymphducts and other recent anatomical discoveries? To deride a doctrine because it does not happen to be mentioned in any ancient author would therefore be absurd, especially bearing in mind this axiom of Logic : locus ab auctoritate negativa non tenet. 42. Fourthly, I premise that Holy Scripture and ecclesiastical tradition do not teach us any thing beyond what is requisite for the salvation of the soul, namely Faith, Hope and Charity. Consequently, from a thing not being stated either by Scripture or tradition it must not be inferred sit, quod illud tale existat : aut nos quidem Fides docet, Deum per Verbum suum omnia creasse visibilia, et invisibilia ; pariterque ex Jesu Christi Domini nostri meritis tum gratiam, tum gloriam omni, et cuivis rationali creaturæ conferri. Num autem alius Mundus a nostro, quem incolimus, sit, et in eo alii homines non ab Adam prognati, sed alio modo a Deo creati existant (sicut ponunt illi qui lunarem globum habitatum opinantur); pariterque num in hoc Mundo, quem incolimus, aliæ existant creaturæ rationales ultra homines, et Spiritus Angelicos, quæ regulariter hominibus sint invisibles, et per accidens, et earum executiva potentia fiant visibles : hoc nullo modo spectat ad fidem, et hoc scire, aut ignorare non est ad salutem hominis necessarium, sicut nec scire rerum omnium physicarum numerum aut naturam. 43. Præmittendum 5 , nullam inveniri repugnantiam, nec in Philosphia, nec in Theologia; quod dari possint creaturæ rationales constantes spiritu et corpore, aliæ ab homine, quia si esset repugnantia, hoc esset vel ex parte Dei (et hoc non quia ipse omnipotens est), vel ex parte rei creabilis ;

that that thing is not in existence. For instance, Faith teaches us that God, by His Word, made things visible, and invisible, and also that, through the merits of our Lord Jesus-Christ, grace and glory are conferred on every rational creature. Now, that there be another World than the one we live in, and that it be people by men not born of Adam but made by God, in some other way, as is implied by those who believe the lunar globe to be inhabited; or further, that in the very World we dwell in, there be other rational creatures besides man and the Angelic Spirits, creatures generally invisible to us and whose being is disclosed but accidentally, through the instrumentality of their own power ; all that has nothing to do with Faith, and the knowledge or ignorance thereof is no more necessary to the salvation of man than knowing the number or nature of all physical things. 43. Fifthly, I premise that neither Philosophy nor Theology is repugnant to the possible existence of rational creatures having spirit and body and distinct from man. Such repugnance could be supported only on God, and that is inadmissible, since he is all-mighty, or on the thing to et neque hoc, quia sicut creatura mere spiritualis, ut Angeli, creata est, et mere materialis, ut Mundus, et partim spiritualis, partim corporea, corporeitate terrestri, et crassa, ut homo, ita creabilis est creatura constans spiritu rationali, et corporeitate minus crassa, sed subtiliore, quam sit homo. Et profecto post Resurrectionem anima Beatorum erit unita corpori glorioso dote subtilitatis donato : ut proinde concludi posset, potuisse Deum creare creaturam rationalem corpoream, cui naturaliter indita sit corporis subtilitas, sicut per gratiam corpori glorioso confertur. 44. Astruitur autem magis talium creaturarum possibilitas ex solutione argumentorum, quæ contra positam conclusionem fieri possunt, pariterque ex responsione ad interrogationes, quæ possunt circa eam formari. 45. Prima interrogatio est, an tales creaturæ dicendæ essent animalea rationalia? Quod si sic, quomodo different ab homine, cum quo communem habetent definitionem?

be made, and that likewise cannot be supported; for, as there are purely spiritual creatures, such as Angels, or merely material, such as the World, or lastly semispiritual and semi-corporeal, of an earthly and gross corporeity, such as man, so there may well be in existence a creature endowed with a rational spirit and a corporeity less gross, more subtile than man's. No doubt, moreover, but that after Resurrection, the souls of the blessed will be united with a glorious and subtile body ; from which may be inferred that God may well have made a rational and corporeal creature whose body naturally enjoys the subtilty which will be conferred by the grace on the glorious body. 44. But, the possible existence of such creatures will be still better set forth by solving the arguments which can be adduced against our conclusion, and replying to the questions it may raise. 45. First question : should such creatures be styled rational animals? And if so, in what do they differ from man, with whom they would have that definition in common?

46. Respondeo quod essent animalia rationalia sensibus et organis corporis prædita, sicut homo : differrent autem ab homonime non solum ratione corporis tenuioris, sed etiam materæ. Homo siquidem ex crassiore elementorum omnium parte, puta ex luto, nempe aqua et terra crassa formatus est, ut constat ex Scriptura, Gen. 2. v. 7.; ista vero formata essent ex subtiliore parte omnium, aut unius, seu alterius elementorum;ut proinde alia essent terrea, alia aquea, alia aerea, el alia ignea ; et ut eorum definitio cum hominis definitione non conveniret, addendum esset definitioni hominis crassa materialitas sui corporis, per quam a dictis aminalibus differret. 47. Secunda interrogatio est, quandonam hujus modi animalia fuissent condita, et num cum brutis producta a terra, aut ab aqua, ut quadrupedia, et aves respective ; an vero a Domino Deo formata, ut fuit homo? 48. Respondeo quod de fide est, quod posito, quod existant de facto, creata sint a principio Mundi : sic enim definitur a

46. I reply : Yes, they would be rational animals, provided with senses and organs even as man; they would, however, differ from man not only in the more subtile nature, but also in the matter of their body. In fact, as is shown by Scripture, man has been made from the grossest of all elements, namely clay, a gross mixture of water and earth : but those creatures would be made from the most subtile part of all elements, or of one or other of them ; thus, some would proceed from earth, others from water, or air, or fire ; and, in order that they should not be defined in the same terms as man, to the definition of the latter should be added the mention of the gross materiality of his body, wherein he would differ from said animals. 47. Second question : At what period would those animals have been originated, and wherefrom? From earth, like the beasts, or from water, like quadrupeds, birds, etc.? Or, on the contrary, would they have been made, like man, by our Lord God? 48. I reply : It is an article of belief, expressly laid down by the Council of Lateran, that whatever is in fact and at

Concilio Lateranensi (Firm. de sum. Trinit. et fide cathol.); nempe quod Deus sua omnipotenti virtute simul ab initio temporis utramque de nihilo condidit creaturam, spiritualem et corporalem. Sub illa etenim Creaturarum generalitate etiam illa etenim animalia essent comprehensa. Quo vero ad eorum formationem, decuisse ipsorum corpus a Deo ministerio Angelorum formatum fuisse, sicut a Deo formatum legimus corpus hominis, quia ipsi copulandus erat spiritus immortalis, quandoquidem spiritus incorporeus et proinde nobilissimus corpori pariter originaliter nobiliori cæteris brutis jungendus erat.
49. Tertia interrogatio, an talia animalia habuissent originem ab uno solo, velut omnes homines ab Adam, an vero plura simul formata essent sicut fuit de cæteris animantibus a terra et aqua productis, in quibus fuerunt mares et foeminæ quæ speciem per generationem conservant? Et si hoc oporteret inter talia animalia esse distinctionem sexus; ipsa nasci, et interire; passionibus sensus affici, nutriri, crescere; et tunc quo alimento vescerentur, esset quærendum ; præterea an vitam socialem ducerent, ut homines ; qua politica regerentur ; num urbes ad habitandum struxissent ;

present, was made in the origin of the world. By His all-mighty virtue, God, from the beginning of time, raised together from nothing both orders of creatures, spiritual and corporeal. Now, those animals also would be included in the generality of creatures. As to their formation, it might be said that God Himself, through the medium of Angels, made their body as he did man's, to which an immortal spirit was to be united. That body being of a nobler nature than that of other animals, it was meet that it should be united to an incorporeal and highly noble spirit. 49. Third question : Would those animals descend from one individual, as all men descend from Adam, or, on the contrary, would many have been made at the same time, as was the case for the other living things issued from earth and water, wherein were males and females for the preservation of the kind by generation? Would there be amongst them a distinction between the sexes? Would they be subject to birth and death, to senses, passions, want of food, power of growth? If so, what their nutrition? Would they lead a social life, as men do? By what laws num artes, studia, possessiones, et bella inter ea essent, sicut est in hominibus. 50. Respondeo : potuit esse quod omnia ab uno, velut homines ab Adam, sint progenita; potuit pariter esse, quod ex iis multi mares, et plures foeminæ fuissent formatæ, a quibus per generationem eorum species essent propagatæ. Ultro admitteremus talia animalia oriri et mori ; mares alios, alias f minas inter ea esse ; passionibus, sensibus agitari velut homines ; nutriri et crescere secundum molem sui corporis ; cibum autem ipsorum non crassum qualem requirit crassities corporis humani, sed substantiam tenuem et vaporosam emanantem per effluvia spirituosa a rebus physicis pollentibus corpusculis maxime volatilibus, ut nidor carnium maxime assatarum, vapor vini, fructuum, florum, aromatum, a quibus, copiosa hujusmodi effluvia usque ad totalem partium subtiliorum ac volatilium evaporationem scaturiunt. Talia autem animalia civilem vitam ducere posse, et inter ea distinctos esse gradus dominantium ac servientium pro conditione naturæ ipsorum, artesque, scientias, ministeria, exercitia, loca, mansiones, ac ruled? Would they build up cities for their dwellings, cultivate the arts and sciences, hold property, and wage war between themselves, as men are wont to? 50. I reply : It may be that all descend from one individual, as men descend from Adam; it may be also that a number of males and females were made initially, who preserved their kind by generation. We will further admit that they are born and die; that they are divided into males and females, and are moved by senses and passions, as men are; that they feed and grow according to the size of their body; their food, however, instead of being gross like that required by the human body, must be delicate and vapoury, emanating through spirituous effluvia from whatever in the physical world abounds with highly volatile corpuscles, such as the flavour of meats, especially of roasts, the fume of wine, the fragrancy of fruit, flowers, aromatics, which evolve an abundance of those effluvia until all their subtile and volatile parts have completely evaporated. To their being able to lead a social life, with distinctions of rank and precedence; to their cultivating the arts and sciences, exercising functions, maintaining armies, alia necessaria ad eorum conservationem, nullan penitus importat repugnantiam. 51. Quarta interrogatio est, qualis esset eorum corporis figuratio, an humanam, an aliam formam, et qualem haberent, et an partes corporis ipsorum haberent ordinem essentialem inter se, ut corpora cæterorum animalium, an vero accidentalem tantum, ut corpora flidarum substantiarum, ut olei, aquæ, nubis, fumi, etc.; et num sustantiæ suarum partium organicarum diversimode constarent, ut organa hominum, in quibus sunt aliæ partes crassissimæ, ut ossa, aliæ minus crassæ, ut cartilagines, aliæ tenues, ut membranæ. 52. Responeo, quod quantum ad figuram corpoream nihil certi affirmare debemus, aut possumus, cum talis figura non sit exacte nobis sensibilis, nec quoad visum, nec quoad tactum, præ sui corporis tenuitate, ac perspicacitate; qualis proinde vere sit, noverent ipsi, aliique, qui substantias immateriales intuitive cognoscere possunt. Quoad congruentiam et probabilitatem dico, illa referre speciem corporis humani, cum aliquo distinctivo a corpore humano, nisi forte ad hoc sufficiat sua building up cities, doing in short whatever is requisite for their preservation, I have in the main no objection. 51. Fourth question : What would their figure be, human or otherwise? Would the ordering of the divers parts of their body be essential, as with other animals, or merely accidental, as with fluid substances, such as oil, water, clouds, smoke, etc.? Would those organic parts consist of various substances, as is the case with the organs of the human body, wherein are to be found very gross parts, such as the bones, others less gross, such as the cartilages, and others slender, such as the membranes? 52. I reply : As regards their figure, we neither can nor should be affirmative, since it escapes our senses, being too delicate for our sight or our touch. That we must leave to themselves, and to such as have the privilege of intuitive acquaintance with immaterial substances. But, so far as probability goes, I say that their figure tallies with the human body, save some distinctive peculiarity, should the very tenuity of their body not be deemed sufficient. I am led to that by the consideration that of all ipsorum tenuitas. Ducor, quia corpus humanum plasmatum a Deo perfectissimum est, inter animalia quæque, et cum cætera bruta in terram sint prona, eo quia anima eorum mortalis est, Deus, ut ait poeta Ovid., Metamorphos.: Os homini sublime dedit c lumque tueri Jussit, et erectos ad sidera tollere vultus ; quia anima hominis immortalis ordinata est ad c lestem mansionem. Cum igitur animalia, de quibus loquimur, spiritum haberent immaterialem, rationalem, ac immortalem, et proinde capacem beatitudinis ac damnationis, congruum est, quod corpus, cui talis spiritus copulatur, simile sit omnium animalium nobilissimo, corpori humano. Ex hac positione sequitur, quod ejus corporis partes ordinem inter se essentialem habere deberent ; nec enim pes capiti, ant ventri manus conjungi deberet : sed congrua membrorum essentiali dispositione ordinata, ut essent idonea ministeriis propriis perficiendis. Quo autem ad partes componentes ipsarum organa, dico quod necessarium esset, ut nonullæ ipsarum essent solidiores, aliæ minus solidæ, aliæ tenues, aliæ tenuissimæ pro necessitate operationis organicæ. Nec contra hanc positionem facile the works of God the human frame is the most perfect, and that whilst all other animals stoop to the ground, because their soul is mortal, God, as Ovid, the poet, says, in his Metamorphoses, Gave man an erect figure, bidding him behold [the heavens And raise his face towards the stars, man's soul having been made immortal for the heavenly abode. Considering that the animals we are speaking of would be gifted with a spirit immaterial, rational and immortal, capable therefore of beatitude and damnation, it is proper to admit that the body to which that spirit is united may be like unto the most noble animal frame, that is to say to the human frame. Whence it follows that in the divers parts of that body there must be an essential order; that the foot, for instance, cannot be an appendage to the head, nor the hand to the belly, but that each organ is in its right place, according to the functions it has to perform. As to the constitutive parts of those organs, it is, in my opinion, necessary that there should be some more or less strong, others more or less slender, in order to meet the requirements of the organic working. Nor can this be fairly potest asseri tenuitas ipsorum corporum : quippe soliditas aut crassities organicarum partium, de qua dicimus, non esset talis simpliciter, sed comparative ad alias partes tenuiores. Et hoc patere potest in omnibus corporibus fluidis naturalibus, ut vino, oleo, lacte, etc.; quantumvis enim omnes partes in ipsis videantur homogeneæ ac similares, non tamen ita est : nam in ipsis est pars terrea, pars aquea, sal fixum, sal volatile, et pars sulfurea, quæ omnia manipulatione spargirica oculis subjici possunt. Ita esset in casu nostro : posito enim quod talium animalium corpora subtilia et tenuia, ut corpora naturalia fluida, velut aqua et aer, essent, non tamen tolleretur, quin in ipsorum partibus diversæ inter se essent qualitates, et aliquæ ipsarum comparative ad alias essent solidæ, et aliæ tenuiores, quamvis totum corpus ex ipsis compositum tenue dici posset. 53. Quod si dicatur, quod hæc repugnant positioni supra firmatæ, circa partium essentialem ordinationem inter se : quoandoquidem videmus, quod in corporibus fluidis ac tenuibus una pars non servat ordinem essentialem ad aliam, sed accidentalem tantum, ita ut hæc par vini, quæ objected to on the ground of the slenderness of the bodies themselves ; for the strength or thickness of the organic parts alluded to would not be absolute, but merely in comparison with the more slender ones. That, moreover, may be observed in all natural fluids, such as wine, oil, milk, etc.; however homogeneous and similar to each other their component parts may look, yet they are not so : for some are clayish, others aqueous ; there are fixed salts, volatile salts, brimstone, all of which are made obvious by a chemical analysis. So it would be in our case : for, supposing the bodies of those animals to be as subtile and slender as the natural fluids, air, water, etc., there would nevertheless be discrepancies in the quality of their constitutive parts, some of which would be strong when compared with others more slender, although the whole body which they compose might be called slender. 53. It may be objected that this is repugnant to what was said above concerning the essential ordering of the parts among themselves ; that it is seen that, in fluid and subtile bodies, one part is not essentially but only accidentally connected with another; that a part of wine, for instance, modo alteri parti contigua est, mox inverso vase, aut moto vino, alteri parti unitur, et sic omnes partes diversam positionem habent quantumvis semper idem vinum sit, et ex hoc sequeretur, quod talium animalium corpora figurata stabiliter non essent, et consequenter, nec organica. 54. Respondeo negando assumptum ; etenim in corporibus fluidis, quamvis non appareat, manet tamen essentialis partium ordinatio, qua stante stat in suo esse compositum, et hoc patet manifeste in vino : expressum enim ab uvis videtur liquor totaliter homogeneus non tamen ita est; in eo enim sunt partes crassæ, quæ tractu temporis subsident in doliis : sunt etiam partes tenues, quæ evaporant : sunt partes fixæ, ut tartarus, sunt partes volatiles, ut sulphur, sive spiritus ardens ; sunt partes mediæ inter volatile ac fixum, ut phlegma. Partes istæ ordinem essentialem inter se mutant ; nam statim ac expressum est ab uvis, et mustum dicitur sulphur, sive spiritus volatilis, ita implicatum manet particulis tartari, qui fixus est, ut nullo modo avolare valeat.

just now contiguous with some other, soon comes in contact with a third, if the vessel be turned upside down or the wine shaken, and that all the parts together exchange positions at the same time, though it be still the same wine. Whence it should be inferred that the bodies of those animals would have no permanent figure, and would consequently not be organic. 54. I reply that I deny the assumption. In fact, if in fluid bodies the essential ordering of the parts is not apparent, it subsists none the less, and causes a compound to preserve its own state. Wine, for instance, when expressed from the grapes, seems a thoroughly homogeneous liquor, and yet is not so ; for there are gross parts which, in the long run, subside in the casks; there are also slender parts which evaporate ; fixed parts, such as tartar ; volatile parts, such as brimstone and alcohol ; others again, half volatile and half fixed, such as phlegm. Those divers parts do not respectively maintain an essential order ; for no sooner has the must been expressed from the grapes, and been styled brimstone or volatile spirits, than it continues so closely involved with the particles of tartar, which is fixed, as not to be in any way able to escape.

55. Hinc est, quod a musto recenter ab uvis expresso nullo modo potest distillari spiritus sulphureus, qui communiter vocatur aqua vitae : sed post quadraginta dies fermentationis particulae vini ordinem mutant, ita ut spiritus , quo alligati erant particulis tartareis, et propria volatilitate eas suspensas tenebant, et vicissim ab eis ne possent avolare detinebantur, ac tartareis particulis separantur, et divulsi ac confusi remanent cum partibus phlegmaticis, a quibus per actionem ignis faciliter separantur, et avolant ; sicque per distillationem fit aqua vitae, quae aliud non est quam sulphur vini volatile cum tenuiore parte phlegmatis simul cum dicto sulphure vi ignis elevata. Post quadraginta dies, alia incipit vini fermentatio, quae longiori, aut minus longo tempore perficitur, pro vini perfectiori aut imperfectiori maturitate, et alio atque alio modo terminatur, pro minore aut majore spiritus sulphurei abundantia. Si enim abundat in vino sulphur, acescit fermentatione, et evadit acetum ; si autem parum sulphuris continet, lentescit vinum, et Italice dicitur vino molle, aut vino guasto. Quod si vinum maturum sit, ut caeteris paribus est, vinum dulce breviori tempore, aut acescit, aut lentescit, ut quotidiana constat experientia. In dicta autem

55. That is the reason why must recently expressed from the grapes is of no use for the distillation of the sulfurous spirits, commonly called brandy ; but, after forty days fermentation, the particles of the wine change places : the spirits, no longer bound with the tartaric particles which they kept in suspension through their own volatility, whilst they were, in return, kept down by them and prevented from escaping, sever from those particles, and continue confused with the phlegmatic parts from which they become easily released by the operation of fire, and evaporate : thus, by means of distillation, brandy is made, which is nothing but the brimstone of wine volatilized by heat with the most slender part of phlegm. At the end of forty days another fermentation begins, which extends more or less, according as the maturity of the wine is more or less perfect, and the termination of which is dependent on the greater or lesser abundance of sulphurous spirits. If abounding with brimstone, the wine sours and turns to vinegar; if, on the contrary, it holds but little brimstone, it ropes, and becomes what the Italians call vino molle or vino guasto. If the wine is at once ripe, as happens in other cases, it sours or ropes in less time,

fermentatione ordo essentialis partium vini mutatur ; non enim ipsius quantitas, aut materia imminuitur, aut mutatur : videmus enim lagenam vino plenam tractu temporis evadere plenam aceto, nullatenus mutatam circa quantitatem materiæ, quæ prius ibi extabat, sed tantum mutato partium essentiali ordine : nam sulphur, quod, ut diximus, erat phlegmati unitum, ac a tartaro separatum, iterum tartaro implicatur, et cum eo fixatur, et proinde si distilletur acetum, primo prodit phlegma insipidum, et post spiritus aceti, qui est sulphur vini illaqueatum particulis tartari minus fixi. Mutatio autem essentialis partium supradictarum variat substantiam liquoris expressi ab uva, quod manifeste patet ex variis et contrariis effectibus, quos causant mustum, vinum, et acetum, et vinum lentum, quod voacatur corruptum, ut proinde duo prima apta materia sint ad consecrationem, secus alia duo. Hanc porro vini economiam hausimus ab erudito opere Nicolai Lemerii, Regis Galliarum aromatarii, Curs. De Chimi., p. 2. c. 9.

as is shown by every day experience. Now, in said fermentation the essential order of the parts of wine is altered, but not so its quantity nor its matter, which neither changes nor decreases : a bottle that had been filled with wine is, after a certain time, found to be filled with vinegar, without any alteration in its quantity of matter; the essential order of its parts has alone been modified : the brimstone, which, as we have said, was united to the phlegm and separated from the tartar, becomes again involved and fixed with the tartar; so that, on distilling the vinegar, there issues from it first an insipid phlegm, and then spirits of vinegar, which are the brimstone of wine intermixed with particles of tartar that is less fixed. Now, the essential shifting of the aforesaid parts alters the substance of the juice of the grapes, as is clearly shown by the varied and contrary effects of must, wine, vinegar, and ropy or spoiled wine; for which cause the two first are fit, but the two last unfit materials for consecration. We have borrowed the above exposition of the economy of wine from the able work of Nicholas Lemery, perfumer to the King of France, Course of Chemistry, p. 2. c. q.

56. Datam ergo naturalem doctrinam applicando consequenter dico, quod data dictorum animalium corporeitate subtili et tenui, sicut corpora liquidorum, et data pariter eorumdem organizatione et figuratione, quæ partium essentialem ordinationem exigunt, non sequerentur inconvenientia ex adverso illata : nam sicut (quemadmodum dicebamus) ex confusione partium vini, et diversa ipsarum accidentali positione non variatur ordinatio earumdem essentialis, ita esset in corpore tenui dictorum animalium. 57. Quinta interrogatio est, an talia obnoxia essent ægritudinibus, ac aliis imperfectionibus, quibus homines laborant, ut ignorantia, metu, segnitie, sensuum impedimentis, etc.? An laborando lassarentur, et ad virium reparationem egerent somno, cibo, ac potu, et quo? et consequenter an interirent, et subinde, an a cæteris animalibus casu, aut ruina possent occidi? 58. Respondeo, quod ex quo corpora ipsorum, quamvis tenuia, essent materiata, essent quidem corruptioni obnoxia; et ex consequenti possent pati ab agentibus contrariis, et ita ægrotare, puta aut simpliciter

56. If now we apply that natural doctrine to our subject, I say that, being given the corporeity of the animals in question, subtile and slender like the substance of liquids ; being given also their organisation an dfigure, which demand an essential order of the various parts, an adverse supposition could raise no argument contrary to their existence ; for, just as the jumbling together of the parts of wine and the diversity of their accidental dispositions do not alter their essential order, even so it would be with the slender frame of our animals. 57. Fifth question : Would those animals be subject to diseases and other infirmities under which mankind lies, such as ignorance, fear, idleness, sensual paralysis, etc? Would they be wearied through labour, and require, for recruiting their strength, sleep, food, drink? And what food, what drink? Would they be fated to die, and might they be killed casually, or by the instrumentality of other animals? 58. I reply : Their bodies, though subtile, being material, they would of course be liable to decay : they might therefore suffer from adverse agencies, and consequently be diseased ; that is, their organs might

aut nisi ægre, perverse, aut vitiose præstare non posse munera, ad quæ eorum organa essent ordinat ; in hoc siquidem consistit animalium quorumdam ægritudo quævis : ut resolutive docet præestantissimus Michael Ettumullerus, Physiol. c. 5., thes. I. Verum est, quod ex eo quod tantam materiæ crassitatem non haberent, et forte ex tot elementorum mixtione eorum corpus non constaret, et minus compostitum esset quam humanum, non tam facile paterentur a contrariis, et consequenter non tot ægritudinibus velut homines essent obnoxia, et longiorem , etiam homine, vitam ducerent : quo enim perfectius est animal, a tota specie, etiam cæteris diutius vivit, ut patet de specie humana, cujus vita longior cæteris animalibus est. Nec enim admitto sæcularem vitam cornicum, cervorum, corvorum et similium, de quibus more suo fabulatur Plinius, et ejus somnia sine prævia discussione secuti sunt cæteri : quandoquidem nullus est, qui talium animalium natale et interitum fideliter adnotaverit, ut pari modo de eo scripserit ; sed insolitam diu fabulam quique secutus est ; sicut etiam illud, quod de ph nice dicitur, quod ut quid fabulosum, circa ejus vitæ spatium recenset Tacitus, l. 6. Annal. Inferendum subinde esset quod illorum animalium vita not perform, or painfully and imperfectly perform the office assigned to them, for therein consist all diseases whatever with certain animals, as has been distinctly explained by the most illustrious Michael Ettmuller, Physiology, c. v. thesis I. In sooth, their body being less gross than the human frame, comprising less elements mixed together, and being therefore less composite, they would not so easily suffer from adverse influences, and would therefore be less liable to disease than man ; their life would also exceed his; for, the more perfect an animal, as a species, the longer its days ; thus mankind, whose existence extends beyond that of other animals. For I do not believe in the centenary existence of crows, stags, ravens and the like, of which Pliny tells his customary stories ; and although his dreams have been reechoed by others without previous inquiry, it is no less clear that before writing thus, not one has faithfully noted the birth nor the death of those animals : they have been content with taking up the strange fable, as has been the case with the Phenix, whose longevity is discarded as a story by Tacitus, Annals, b. 6. It were therefore to be inferred that the animals we are speaking of would live longer still than man ; for, as etiam humana deberet esse diuturnior : ut enim infra dicemus, illa esset homine nobiliora ; consequenter dicendum esset, quod essent obnoxia cæteris corporeis pathematis, et quiete, et cibo indigerent, quale diximus supra, n 50. Quia vero rationalia, et proinde disciplinabilia essent, ex consequenti etiam capacia ignorantiæ, si eorum ingenia non essent exculta studiis, et disciplina, et inter ea pro intellectus eorum majori, et minori acumine essent aliqua magis, aliqua minus in scientiis excellentia : universaliter vero, et a tota specie essent homine doctiora, non ob eorum corpoream subtilitatem, tum forte, ob majorem spirituum activitatem, tum ob diuturniorem vitæ durationem, in qua plura, quam homines discere possent, quas causas assignat D .Augustinus, lib. de Diven. Dæm. c. 3. init. tom. 3., et lib. de Spir. et Anima, c. 37., pro futurorum prænotione in Dæmonibus. Ab agentibus autem naturalibus pati quidem possent, ac difficulter occidi ratione velocitatis, qua possunt se subtrahere a nocentibus ; quapropter, nec a brutis, nec ab homine armis naturalibus, seu artificialibus nisi maxima difficultate possent occidi, aut mutilari, et maxima eorumdem velocitate in declinando contrarium impetum. Possent vero in sommo shall be said below, they would be more noble than he ; consequently also, they would be subject to the other bodily affections, and require rest and food, as mentioned, number 50. Now, as rational beings amenable to discipline, they might also continue ignorant, if their minds did not receive the culture of study and instruction, and some amongst them would be more or less versed in science, more or less clever, according as their intelligence had been more or less trained. However, generally speaking, and considering the whole of the species, they would be more learned than men, not from the subtilty of their body, but perhaps because of the greater activity of their mind or the longer space of their life, which would enable them to learn more things than men : such are indeed the motives assigned by S. Austin (Divin. Demon. ch. 3. and Spirit and Soul, ch. 37), to the prescience of the future in Demons. They might indeed suffer from natural agencies ; but they could hardly be killed, on account of the speed with which they could escape from danger ; it is therefore most unlikely that they could, without the greatest difficulty, be put to death or mutilated by beast or by man, with natural or artificial weapons, so quick would they be aut in non advertentia occidi, et mutilati a corpore solido, ut ense vibrato ab homine, aut lapide delapso per ruinam, quia eorum corpus licet tenue, tamen et quantum, et divisibile esset, velut aer qui ferro, fuste, aut alio corpore solido dividitur quamvis tenuis sit. Eorum autem spiritus impartibilis esset, et ceu anima hominis totus in toto, et totus in quavis corporis parte. Hinc fieret quod diviso corpore ipsorum, ut præfertur, per aliud corpus, sequi posset mutilatio, et proinde etiam mors : non enim fieri posset ut diviso corpore idem spiritus utramque partem informaret, cum ipse indivisibilis esset. Verum est quod sicut partes aeris divisæ , per intermedium corpus, hoc sublato iterum uniuntur, et evadit idem aer, possent pariter partes corporis divisæ, ut supra ponitur, reuniri, et ab eodem spiritu revivificari. Sed hoc modo nequirent talia animalia ab agentibus naturalibus aut artificialibus occidi : sed rationabilior esset prima positio ; ex hoc enim, quod communicarent cum cæteros in materia, æquum est, ut a cæteris etiam usque ad eorum interitum pati possent, ut fit cum cæteris.

at avoiding the impending blow. Yet, they might be killed or mutilated in their sleep, or in a moment of inadvertence, by means of a solid body, such as a sword brandished by a man, or the fall of a heavy stone ; for, although subtile, their body would be divisible, just like air which, though vaporous, is yet divided by a sword, a club, or any other solid body. Their spirit, however, would be indivisible, and like the human soul, entire in the whole and in each and every part of the body. Consequently, the division of their body by another body, as aforesaid, might occasion mutilation and even death, for the spirit, itself indivisible, could not animate both parts of a divided body. True, just as the parts of air, separated by the agency of a body, unite again as soon as that body is withdrawn, and constitute the same air as before, even so the parts of the body divided, as above-mentioned, might unite and be revived by the same spirit. But then, it must be inferred that those animals could not be slain by natural or artificial agencies : and it were more rational to keep to our first position; for, if sharing matter with other creatures, it is natural that they should be liable to suffer through those creatures, according to the common rule, and even unto death.

59. Sexta interrogatio est, an ipsorum corpora possent alia corpora penetrare, ut parietes, ligna, metalla, vilrum, etc., et an multa ipsorum possent in eodem loco materiali consistere, et ad quantum spatium extederetur, seu restringeretur eorum corpus? 60. Respondeo, quod cum in omnibus corporibus quantumvis compactis dentur pori, ut ad sensum patet in metallis, de quibus major esset ratio, quod in ipsis non darentur pori : microscopio perfecte elaborato discernuntur pori metallorum, cum suis diversis figuris, utique possent per poros insinuari quibusvis corporibus, et hoc modo ista penetrare, quantumvis tales pori penetrari non possent ab alio liquore, aut spiritu materiali, aut vini, salis ammoniaci, aut similium, quia lonte tenuiora essent istis liquoribus illorum corpora. Quamvis autem plures Angeli possint esse in eodem loco materiali, et etiam restringi ad locum minorem minore non tamen in infinitum, ut probat Scotus in 2. dist. 2. q. 6. § Ad proposi. et quæst. 8., per totum, hoc tamen concedendum non esset de corposibus talium animalium ; tum quia corpora ipsa essent quanta, et eorum dimensio non esset reciproce penetrabilis; tum

59. Sixth question : Could their bodies penetrate other bodies, such as walls, wood, metals, glass, etc? Could many of them abide together on the same material spot, and to what space would their body extend or be restrained? 60. I reply : In all bodies, however compact, there are pores, as is apparent in metals where, more than in other bodies, it would seem there should be none ; through a perfect microscope the pores of metals are discerned, with their different shapes. Now, those animals might, through the pores, creep into, and thus penetrate any other bodies, although such pores were impervious to other liquors or material spirits, of wine, ammoniacal salt, or the like, because their bodies would be much more subtle than those liquors. However, notwithstanding many Angels may abide together on the same material spot, and even confine themselves in a lesser and lesser space, though not infinitely, as is shown by Scott, yet it were rash to ascribe the same power to those animals ; for, their bodies are determined in substance and impervious to each other ; and if two glorious bodies cannot abide

quia si duo corpora gloriosa non possunt esse in eodem loco, quamvis possent simul esse gloriosum, et non gloriosum, ut voluit Gotofredus de Fontibus, quodlibet 6. q. 5., a quo non discordat Scotus in 2. distinct. 2. q. 8. in fine ; multo minus possent simul esse istorum corpora, quæ, licet subtilia, non tamen æquarent subtilitatem corporis gloriosi. Quo autem ad extensionem et restrictionem, dicendum esset, quod sicut ex rarefactione, et condensatione, majus aut minus spatium oaccupatur ab aere, qui etiam arte potest constringi, ut in minori loco contineatur, quam sit suæ quantitati naturaliter debitus, ut patet in magnis pilis lusoriis, quæ per fistulam seu tubum inflatorium inflantur : in his siquidem aer violenter immittitur, et constringitur, et ejus major ibi continetur quantitas, quam naturalis pilæ capacitas exigat ; ita pariformiter talia corpora ex ipsorum naturali virtute possent ad majus spatium, non tamen excedens eorum quantitatem, extendi : ut pariter etiam restringi, non tamen circa determinatum locum suæ quantitati debitum. Et quia ipsorum nonnulla, prout etiam in hominibus est, essent magna, et nonnulla parva, congruum esset, ut magna possent plus extendi, quam parva, et hæc ad minorem locum restringi, quam magna.

together on the same spot, though a glorious and a non glorious one may do so, according to some Doctors, much less would it be possible for the bodies of those animals, which are indeed subtile, yet do not attain to the subtility of the glorious body. As regards their power of extension or compression, we may instance the case of air, which, rarefied and condensed, occupies more or less room, and may even, by artificial means, be compressed into a narrower space than would be naturally due to its volume; as is seen with those large balls which, for amusement, one inflates by means of a blow-pipe or tube : air, being forced into them and compressed, is held in larger quantity than is warranted by the capacity of the ball. Similarly the bodies of the animals we are speaking of might, by their natural virtue, extend to a larger space, not exceeding however their own substance ; they might also contract, but not beyond the determined space due to that same substance. And, considering that of their number, as with men, some would be tall and some short, it were proper that the tall should be able to extend more than the short, and the short to contract more than the tall.

61. Septima interrogatio est, an hujusmodi animalia in peccato originali nascerentur, et a Christo Domino fuissent redempata ; an ipsis conferretur gratia, et per quæ sacramenta ; sub qua lege viverent, et an beatitudinis et danmatiois essent caacia? 62. Respondeo, quod articulus Fidei est, quod Christus Dominus pro universa creatura rationali gratiam et gloriam meruit. Pariter articulus Fidei est, quod Creaturæ rationali gloria non confertur nisi præcedat in ea gratia, quæ est dispsitio ad gloriam. Similis articulus est quod gloria non confertur nisi per merita. Hæc vero fundatur in observantia perfecta mandatorum Dei adimpleta per gratiam. Ex his satis fit positis interrogationibus. Incertum est an tales Creaturæ originaliter peccavissent, necne. Certum tamen est, quod si ipsarum Prothoparens peccasset, sicut peccavit Adam, ipsius descendentes in peccato originali nascerentur, quemadmodum nascuntur homines.Et quia Deus nunquam reliquit Creaturam rationalem sine remedio, dum ipsa est in via ; si hujusmodi creaturæ in peccato originali, aut actuali inficerentur, Deus providisset illis de remedio, sed quale sit, an fecisset, noverit Deus, noverint

61. Seventh question : Would those animals be born in original sin, and have been redeemed by the Lord Christ? Would the grace have been conferred upon them and through what sacraments? Under what law would they live, and would they be capable of beatitude and damnation? 62. I reply : It is an article of belief that Christ has merited grace and glory for all rational creatures without exception. It is also an article of belief that glory is not conferred on a rational creature until such creature has been previously endowed with grace, which is the disposition to glory. According to a like article, glory is conferred but by merits. Now, those merits are grounded on the perfect observance of the commands of God, which is accomplished through grace. The above questions are thus solved. Whether those creatures did or did not sin originally is uncertain. It is clear, however, that if their first Parent had sinned as Adam sinned, his descent would be born in original sin, as men are born. And, as God never leaves a rational creature without a remedy, so long as it treads the way, if those creatures were infected with original or with actual sin, God would have provided them with a

ipsæ. Hoc certum est, si inter ipsas essent eadem, aut alia sacramenta, ac sunt in Ecclesia humana militanti, ipsa habuissent, et institutionem, et efficaciam a meritis Jesu Christi, qui omnium creaturarum rationalium Redemptor et Satisfactor universalis est. Convenientissimum pariter, immo necessarium esset quod sub aliqua lege a Deo sibi data viverent, ut per ipsius observantiam possent sibi beatitudinem mereri ; quænam autem lex fuisset, an naturalis tantum, aut scripta, Mosaica aut Evangelica, aut alia ab his omnibus differens, prout Deo placuisset, hoc nobis incognitum. Quoquomodo autem fuisset, nulla resultaret repugnantia possibilitatem talium creaturarum excludens. 63. Unicum porro argumentum, et quidem satis debile post longam meditationem mihi subit contra talium creaturarum possibilitatem : et est quod si tales creaturæ in Mundo existerent, de ipsis notitia aliqua tradita fuisset a Philosophis, Sacra Scriptura, Traditione Ecclesiastica, aut Sanctis Patribus ; quod cum non fuerit, tales creaturas minime possibiles esse concludendum est.

remedy ; but whether it is the case, and of what kind is the remedy, is a secret between God and them. Surely, if they had sacraments identical with or different from those in use in the human Church militant, for the institution and efficacy thereof they would be indebted to the merits of Jesus-Christ, the Redeemer and universal Atoner of all rational creatures. It would likewise be highly proper, nay necessary, that they should live under some law given them by God, and through the observance of which they might merit beatitude ; but what would be that law, whether merely natural or written, Mosaic or Evangelical, or different from all these and specially instituted by God, that we are ignorant of. Whatever it might be though, there would follow no objection exclusive of the possible existence of such creatures.

63. The only argument, and that a rather lame one, which long meditations has suggested to me against the possibility of such creatures, is that, if they really existed in the World, we should find them mentioned somewhere by Philosophers, Holy Scripture, Ecclesiastical Tradition, or the Holy Fathers : such not being the case, their utter impossibility should be inferred.

64. Sed hoc argumentum, quod revera magis pulsat existentiam, quam possibilitatem illarum, facili negotio solvitur ex iis quæ præmissimus supra n 41. et 42. Argumentum enim ab auctoritate negativa non tenet. Præterquam quod falsum est, quod de illis notitiam non tradiderint tum Philosophi, tum Scriptura, tum Patres. Plato siquidem, ut refert Apuleius de Deo Socratis et Plutarchus de Isid. apud Baronem,Scot. Defens., tom. 9. Apparant. p. I. fol. 2., voluit Dæmones esse animalia genere, animo passiva, mente rationalia, corpore aerea, tempore æterna : creaturasque istas nomine Dæmonum intitulavit ; quod tamen nomen non male sonat ex se : importat enim plenum sapientia; unde cum Diabolum (Angelum nempe malum) volunt auctores exprimere, non simpliciter Dæmonem sed Cacadæmonem vocant : sicut Eudæmonem, quando bonum Angelum volunt intelligi. Similiter in Scriptura Sacra et Patribus, de dictis creaturis habetur mentio, et de hoc infra dicemus. 65. Stabilita huc usque talium creaturarum possibilitate, ad earumdem existentiam probandam descendamus. Supposita tot historiarum veritate de coitu hujusmodi Incuborum et Succuborum cum hominibus

64. But that argument which, in fact, calls in question their existence rather than their possibility, is easily disposed of by our premises, Nrs 41 and 42; for no argument can stand in virtue of a negative authority. Besides, it is not correct to assert that neither the Philosophers, nor the Scriptures, nor the Fathers have handed down any notion of them. Plato, as is reported by Apuleius (The Demon of Socrates) and Plutarch (Isis and Osiris), declared that Demons were beings of the animal kind, passive souls, rational intelligences, aerial bodies, everlasting; and he gave them the name of Demons, which of itself is nowise offensive, since it means replete with wisdom; so that, when authors allude to the Devil (or Evil Angel), they do not merely call him Demon, but Cacodemon, and say likewise Eudemon, when speaking of a good Angel. Those creatures are also mentioned in Scripture and by the Fathers, as shall be said hereafter. 65. Now that we have proved that those creatures are possible, let us go a step further, and show that they exist. Taking for granted the truth of the recitals concerning the intercourse of Incubi and Succubi

et brutis, ita ut hoc negare impudentia videatur, ut ait D. Augustinus quem dedimus supra n 10., ita arguo : Ubi reperitur propria passio sensus, ibidem necessario reperitur sensus ipse, cum juxta principia philosophica propria passio fluat a natura, sive ubi reperiuntur actiones seu operationes sensus, ibidem reperitur sensus ipse, cum operationes et actines sint a forma. Atqui in hujusmodi Incubis aut Succubis, sunt actiones, operationes, ac propiæ passiones, quæ sunta a sensibus ; ergo in iisdem repritur sensus : sed sensus reperini nequit nisi adsint organa composita, nempe ex potentia animæ et determinata parte corporis : ergo in iisem reperiuntur corpus et anima ; erunt igitur animalia : sed etiam in ipsis et ab ipsis sunt actiones, et operationes animæ rationalis : ergo eorum anima erit rationalis : et ita de primo ad ultimum tales Incubi sunt animalia rationalia. 66. Minor probatur quoad singulas ejus partes. Passio siquidem appetitiva coitus est passio sensus; moeror, ac tristitia, ac iracundia et furor ex coitu denegato passiones sensus sunt, ut patet in quibusvis with men and beasts, recitals so numerous that it would look like impudence to deny the fact, as is said by St Austin, whose testimony is given above (Nr 10), I argue : Where the peculiar passion of the sense is found, there also, of necessity, is the sense itself; for, according to the principles of philosophy, the peculiar passion flows from nature, that is to say : that, where the acts and operations of the sense are found, there also is the sense, the operations and acts being but its external form. Now, those Incubi and Succubi present acts, operations, peculiar passions, which spring from the senses; they are therefore endowed with senses. But senses cannot exist without concomitant composite organs, without a combination of soul and body. Incubi and Succubi have therefore body and soul, and, consequentially, are animals; but their acts and operations are also those of a rational soul; their soul is therefore rational; and thus, from first to last, they are rational animals. 66. Our minor is easy of demonstration in each of its parts. And indeed, the appetitive passion of coition is a sensual passion; the grief, sadness, wrath, rage, occasioned by the denial of coition, are sensual passions, animalibus; generatio per coitum est operatio sensus, ut notum est. Hæc porro omnia in Incubis sunt : ut enim probavimus supra a n 25. et seq., ipsi coitum muliebrem, et quandoque virilem appetunt, tritantur, et furunt, ut amantes, amentes, si ipsis denegetur ; coeunt perfecte et quandoque generant. Concludendum ergo quod polleant sensu, et proinde corpore; unde inferendum etiam perfecta animalia esse. Pariter clausis ostiis ac fenetris intrant ubivis locorum : igitur ipsorum corpus tenue est; item futura prænoscunt, annuntiant, componunt, ac dividunt ; quæ operationes sunt propiæ animæ rationalis : ergo anima rationali pollent ; et ita sunt vera animalia rationalia. Respondent communiter Doctores, quod malus Dæmon est ille qui tales impudicitias operatur, quod passiones, nempe amorem, tristitiamque simulant ex coitu denegato, ut animas ad peccandum alliciat, et eas perdat; et si coit, et generat, hoc est ex semine, et in corpore alieno, ut dictum fuit supra n 24. 67. Sed contra Incubi nonnulli rem habent cum equis, equabus, aliisque etiam brutis, quæ si coitum adversentur, male ab ipsis tractantur, ut quotidiana constat experientia;

as is seen with all animals ; generation through coition is evidently a sensual operation. Now, all that happens with Incubi, as has been shown above : they incite women, sometimes even men; if denied, they sadden and storm, like lovers : amantes, amentes ; they perfectly practice coition, and sometimes beget. It must therefore be inferred that they have senses, and consequently a body ; consequently also, that they are perfect animals. More than that : with closed doors and windows they enter wherever they please : their body is therefore slender; they foreknow and foretell the future, compose and divide, all which operations are proper to a rational soul ; they therefore possess a rational soul and are, in sooth, rational animals. Doctors generally retort that it is the Evil Spirit that perpetrates those impure acts, simulates passions, love, grief at the denial of coition, in order to entice souls to sin and to undo them; and that, if he copulates and begets, it is with assumed sperm and body, as aforesaid (Nr 24). 67. But then, there are Incubi that have to do with horses, mares and other beasts, and, as shown by every day experience, illtreat them if rebel to coition ; yet, in those sed in istis cessat ratio adducta, nempe quod fingat appetitum coitus, ut animas perdat, cum anima brutorum damnationis æternæ sit incapax. Præterea amoris et iræ passiones in ipso contrarios effectus reales producunt. Si enim aut mulier aut brutum amatum illis morem gerant, optime ab Incubis tractantur ; viceversa pessime habentur, si ex denegato coitu irascantur et furant ; et hoc firmatur quotidiana experientia ; ergo in ipsis sunt veroæ passiones sensus. Insuper mali Dæmones, ac incorporei, qui rem habent cum Sagis et Maleficis, ipsas cogunt ad eorum adorationem, ad denegandam Fidem Orthodoxam, ad maleficia et scelera enormia perpetranda tanquam pensum infamis coitus, ut supra n II. dictum fuit : nihil horum prætendunt Incubi, ergo mali Dæmones non sunt. Ulterius malus Dæmon, ut ex Peltano et Thyreo scribit Guaccius, Compend. Malef. lib. I. c. 19. fol. 128., ad prolationem nominis Jesu aut Mariæ, ad formationem signi Crucis, ad approximationem sacrarum Reliquiarum , sive rerum benedictarum, et ad exorcismos, adjurationes, aut præcepta sacerdotum, aut fugit aut pavet, concutiturque, et stridet, ut conspicitur quotidie in energumenis, et constat ex tot historiis, quas recitat cases, it can no longer be adduced that the Demon simulates the appetite for coition in order to bring about the ruin of souls, since those of beasts are not capable of everlasting damnation. Besides, love and wrath with them are productive of quite opposite effects. For, if the loved woman or beast humours them, those Incubi behave very well; on the contrary, they use them most savagely when irritated and enraged by a denial of coition : this is amply proved by daily experience : those Incubi therefore have truly sexual passions. Besides, the Evil Spirits, the incorporeal Demons which have to do with Sorceresses and Witches, constrain them to Demon-Worship, to the abjuration of the Orthodox Faith, to the commission of enchantments and foul crimes, as preliminary conditions to the infamous intercourse, as has been above-stated (Nr I I); now, Incubi pretend to nothing of the kind : they are therefore no Evil Spirits. Lastly, as written by Guaccius, at the mere utterance of the name of Jesus or Mary, at the sign of the Cross, the approach of Holy Relics or consecrated objects, at exorcisms, adjurations or priestly injunctions, the Evil Demon either shudders and takes to flight, or is agitated and howls, as is daily seen with

Guaccius, ex quibus habetur, quod in nocturnis ludis Sagarum facto ab aliquo assistentium signo Crucis, aut pronuntiato nomine Jesu, Diaboli et secum Sagæ omnes disparuerunt. Sed Icubi ad supradicta nec fugiunt, nec pavent, quandoque cachinnis exorcismos excipiunt, et quandoque ipsos Exorcistas cædunt, et sacras vestes discerpuent. Quod si mali Dæmones, utpote a D. N. J. C domiti, ad ipsius nomen, Crucem, et res sacras pavent : boni autem Angeli eisdem rebus gaudent, non tamen homines ad peccata et Dei offensam sollicitant : Incubi vero sacra non timent, et ad peccata provocant, convincitur ipsos nec malos Dæmones, nec bones Angelos esse; sed patet, quod nec homines sunt, cum tamen ratione utantur. Quid ergo erunt? Si in termino termno sunt, et simplices spiritus sunt, erunt aut damnati aut beati : non enim in bona Theologia dantur puri spiritus viatores. Si damnati, nomen et Crucem Christi revererentur ; si beati, homines ad peccandum non provocarent ; ergo aliud erunt a puris spiritus; et sic erunt corporati, et viatores.

energumens and is shown by numerous narratives of Guaccius concerning the nightly revels of Witches, where, at a sign of the Cross or the name of Jesus said by one of the assistants, Devils and Witches all vanish together. Incubi, on the contrary, stand all those ordeals without taking to flight or showing the least fear; sometimes even they laugh at exorcisms, strike the Exorcists themselves, and rend the sacred vestments. Now, if the evil Demons, subdued by our Lord Jesus-Christ, are stricken with fear by his name, the Cross and the holy things; if, on the other hand, the good Angels rejoice at those same things, without however inciting men to sin nor to give offense to God, whilst the Incubi, without having any dread of the holy things, provoke to sin, it is clear that they are neither evil Demons nor good Angels ; but it is clear also that they are not men, though endowed with reason. What then should they be? Supposing them to have reached the goal, and to be pure spirits, they would be damned or blessed, for correct Theology does not admit of pure spirits on the way to salvation. If damned, they would revere the name and the Cross of Christ; if blessed, they would not incite men to sin ; they would therefore be different

68. Præterea agens materiale non potest agere nisi in passum similiter materiale; tritum siquidem est axioma philosophorum, quod agens et patiens debent communicare in subjecto ; nec id quod materiatum est, potest agere in rem pure spiritualem. Dantur autem agentia naturalia, quæ agunt contra hujusmondi Dæmones Incubos, sequitur igitur quod isti materiati, seu corporei sunt. Minor probatur ex iis quæ scribunt Dioscorides, l. 2. c. 168. et l. I c.100.,Plinius, lib. 15. c. 4., Aristoteles, Probl. 34., et Apuleius, l. De Virtute Herbarum, apud Guaccium, Comp. Malef., l. 3. c. 13. fol. 316., et confirmatur experientia, nempe de pluribus herbis, lapidibus ac animalibus, quæ Dæmones depellunt, ut ruta, hypericon, verbena, scordium, palma Christi, centaureum, adamas, corallium, gagates, jaspis, pellis capitis lupi aut asini, menstruum muliebre, et centum alia ; unde habetur 26, q. 7. cap. final.: Dæmonium sustinenti liceat petras, vel herbas habere sine incantatione. Ex quo habetur, petras aut herbas posse sua vi naturali Dæmonis vires compescere, aliter Canon hoc non permitteret, sed ut superstitiosum

from pure spirits, and thus, have a body and be on the way to salvation. 68. Besides, a material agent cannot act but on an equally material passive. It is indeed a trite philosophical axiom, that agent and patient must have a common subject : pure matter cannot act on any purely spiritual thing. Now, there are natural agents which act on those Incubi Demons : these are therefore material or corporeal. Our minor is proved by the testimony of Dioscorides, Pliny, Aristoteles and Apuleius, quoted by Guaccius, Comp. Malef. b. 3, ch. 13, fol. 316; it is confirmed by our knowledge of numerous herbs, stones and animal substances which have the virtue of driving away Demons, such as rue, St-John's wort, verbena, germander, palma Christi, centaury, diamonds, coral, jet, jasper, the skin of the head of a wolf or an ass, women's catamenia, and a hundred others : wherefore it is written : For such as are assaulted by the Demon it is lawful to have stones or herbs, but without recourse to incantations. It follows that, by their own native virtue, stones or herbs can bridle the Demon : else the above mentioned Canon would not permit their use, but would on the contrary forbid it as vetaret. Et he hoc luculentum exemplum habemus in Sacra Scriptura, ubi Angelus Raphael dixit Tobiæ, c. 6, v. 8. : Cordis ejus (nempe piscis, quem a Tigri attraxerant) particulam, si super carbones ponas, fumus ejus extricat omne genus Dæmoniorum. Et ejus virtuten experientia comprobavit : nam incenso jecore piscis, fugatus est Incubus, qui Saram deperiebat. 69. Respndent ad hæc communiter Theologi, quod talia agentia naturalia inchoative tantum fugant Dæmonem, completive autem vis supernaturalis Dei aut Angeli, ita ut virtus supernaturalis sit causa primaria, directa, et principalis,naturalis autem secondaria, indirecta, et minus principalis. Unde ad probationem, quæ supra adducta est de Dæmone fugato a fumo jecoris piscis incensi a Tobia, respondet Vallesius, De Sac. Philosoph., c. 28., quod tali fumo indita fuit a Deo vis supernaturalis fugandi Incubum, sicut igni materiali Inferni data est virtus torquendi Dæmones et animas Damnatorum. Ad eamdem autem probationem respondet Lyranus, et Cornelius ad c. 6. Tob. v. 8., superstitious. We have a striking instance thereof in Holy Scripture, where the Angel Raphael says to Tobit, ch. 6, v. 8, speaking of the fish which he had drawn from the Tigris : "If thou puttest on coals a particle of its liver, the smoke thereof will drive away all kinds of Demons." Experience demonstrated the truth of those words; for, no sooner was the liver of the fish set on fire, than the Incubus who was in love with Sarah was put to flight. 69. To this Theologians usually retort that such natural agents merely initiate the ejection of the Demon, and that the completive effect is due to the supernatural force of God or of the Angel; so that the supernatural force is the primary, direct and principal cause, the natural force being but secondary, indirect and subordinate. Thus, in order to explain how the liver of the fish burnt by Tobit drove away the Demon, Vallesius asserts that the smoke thereof had been endowed by God with the supernatural power of expelling the Incubus, in the same manner as the material fire of Hell has the virtue of tormenting Demons and the souls of the Damned. Others, such as Lyranus and Cornelius,

Abulentis in I. Reg. c. 16. q. 46., Pererius in Daniel., pag. 272., apud Cornel. loc. cit., fumum cordis piscis expulisse Dæmonem inchoate vi naturali, sed complete vi angelica et cælesti : naturali autem impediendo actionem Dæmonis per dispositionem contrariam, quia hic agit per naturales causes et humores, quorum qualitates expugnantur a qualitatibus contrariis rerum naturalium, quæ dicuntur Dæmones fugare ; et in eadem sententia sunt omnes loquentes de arte exorcista. 70. Sed hæc responsio, que tamen validas habet instantias, ad plus quadrare potest contra malos Dæmones obsidentes corpora, aut per maleficia inferentes ipsis ægritudines, aut alia incommoda, sed nullo modo facit ad propositum de Incubis : siquidem isti nec corpora obsident, nec ipsis officiunt per ægritudines habituales, sed ad plus ictibus et percussionibus torquent. Quod si equas coitum adversantes macras reddunt, hoc faciunt subducendo illis cibum, et hoc modo macrescere, et tandem interire eas faciunt. Ad hæc autem patranda non eget Incubus alicujus rei naturalis applicatione (qua tamen eget malus Dæmon inferens agritudinem habitualem), ea enim potest ex sua vi organica naturali. Pariter Dæmon profess that the smoke of the heart of the fish initiated the ejection of the Demon by native virtue, but completed it by angelical and heavenly virtue : by native virtue, insomuch that it opposed a contrary action to that of the Demon; for the Evil Spirit applies native causes and humours, the native qualities of which are combated by the contrary qualities of natural things known to be capable of driving away Demons; that opinion is shared by all those who treat of the art of exorcisms. 70. But that explanation, however plausible the facts upon which it rests, can at most be received as regards the Evil Spirits which possess bodies or, through malefice, infect them with diseases or other infirmities ; it does not at all meet the case of Incubi. For, these neither possess bodies nor infect them with diseases; they, at most, molest them by blows and ill-treatment. If they cause the mares to grow lean because of their not yielding to coition, it is merely by taking away their provender, in consequence of which they fall off and finally die. To that purpose the Incubus need not use a natural agent, as the Evil Spirit does when imparting a disease : it is enough that it should exert its own native organic

malus plerumque obsidet corpora, et infert ægritudines ad signa cum ipso conventa et posita a Saga aut Malefico, quæ signa multoties res naturales sunt præditoæ vi nativa nocendi, quibus naturaliter resistunt alia pariter naturalia contrariæ virtutis. Incubus vero non sic; quia ex se, et nulla concurrente aut Saga, aut Malefico, suas vexationes infert. Præterea res naturales fugantes Incubos suam virtutem exercent, ac effectum sortiuntur absque interventu alicujus exorcismi aut sacræ benedictionis; ut proinde dici non possit, quod fuga Incubi inchoative sit a virtute naturali, completive autem a vi divina, quia ibi nulla particularis intervenit divini nominis invocatio, sed est purus effectus rei naturalis, ad quem non concurrit Deus, nisi concursu universali, tanquam auctor naturæ, et causa universalis, et prima in ordine efficentium.
71. Duas circa hoc historia do, quarum primam habui a Confessario Molinalium, viro gravi ac fide dignissimo. Alterius vero sum testis oculatus.

force. Likewise, when the Evil Spirit possesses bodies and infects them with diseases, it is most frequently through signs agreed upon with himself, and arranged by a witch or a wizard, which signs are usually natural objects, indued with their own noxious virtue, and of course opposed by other equally natural objects endowed with a contrary virtue. But not so the Incubus : it is of his own accord, and without the cooperation of either witch or wizard, that he inflicts his molestations. Besides, the natural things which put the Incubi to flight exert their virtue and bring about a result without the intervention of any exorcism or blessing; it cannot therefore be said that the ejection of the Incubus is initiated by natural, and completed by divine virtue, since there is in this case no particular invocation of the divine name, but the mere effect of a natural object, in which God cooperates only as the universal agent, the author of nature, the first of efficient causes. 71. To illustrate this subject, I give two stories, the first of which I have from a Confessor of Nuns, a man of weight, and most worthy of credit; the second I was eye-witness to.

In quodam Sanctimonalium monasterio degebat ad educationem Virgo quædam nobilis tentata ab Incubo, qui diu noctuque ipsi apparebat, ipsam ad coitum sollicitando eniximis precibus, tamquam amasius præ amore dementatus ; ipsa tamen semper restitit tentati gratia Dei, ac sacramentorum frequentia roborata. Incassum abiere plures devotiones, jejunia et vota facta a puella vexata, exorcismi, benedictiones, et præcepta ab exorcistis facta Incubo, ut desisteret a molestia illa ; nec quidquam proficiebatur multitudo reliquiarum, aliarumque rerum benedictarum disposita in camera virginis tentatæ, nec benedictæ candelæ noctu ibidem ardentes impediebant, quominus juxta consuetum appareret ad tentandum in forma speciosissimi juvenis. Consultus inter alios viros doctos fuit quidam Theologus magnæ eruditionis : iste advertens virginem tentatam esse temperamenti phlegmatici a toto, conjectavit Incubum esse dæmonem aqueum (dantur enim ut scribit Guaccius, Comp. Malefic. l. I. c. 19. fol. 129., Dæmones ignei, aerei, phlegmatici, terrei, subterranei, et lucifugi), et consului, quod in camera virginis tentatæ continue fieret suffimentum vaporosum sequens. Requirunt ollam novam figulinam vitreatam ; in hac ponitur calami

In a certain monastery of holy Nuns there lived, as a boarder, a young maiden of noble birth, who was tempted by an Incubus that appeared to her by day and by night, and with the most earnest entreaties, the manners of a most passionate lover, incessantly incited her to sin ; but she, supported by the grace of God and the frequent use of the sacraments, stoutly resisted the temptation. But, all her devotions, fasts and vows notwithstanding, despite the exorcisms, the blessings, the injunctions showered by exorcists on the Incubus that he should desist from molesting her; in spite of the crowd of relics and other holy objects collected in the maiden's room, of the lighted candles kept burning there all night, the Incubus none the less persisted in appearing to her as usual, in the shape of a very handsome young man. At last, among other learned men, whose advice had been taken on the subject, was a very erudite Theologian who, observing that the maiden was of a thoroughly phlegmatic temperament, surmised that Incubus was an aqueous Demon (there are in fact, as is testified by Guaccius, igneous, aerial, phlegmatic, earthly, subterranean demons who avoid the light of day), and prescribed an uninterrupted aromatici, cubebarum seminis, aristolochiæ utriusque radicum, cardamomi majoris et minoris, gingibeis, piperis longi, caryophyllorum, cinnamomi, canellæ caryophyllatæ, macis, nucum myristicarum, styracis calamitæ, benzoini, ligni ac radicis rodiæ, ligni aloes, triasantalorum una uncia, semiaquæ vitæ libræ tres ; ponitur olla supra cineres calidas ut vapor suffimenti ascendat, et cella clausa tenetur. Facto suffimento advenit denuo Incubus, sed ingredi cellam nunquam ausus est : sed si tentata extra eam ibat, et per viridarium ac claustra spatiabatur, aliis invisibilis sibi visus apparebat Incubus, et puellæ collo injectis brachiis violenter, ac quasi furtive oscula rapiebat : quod molestissimum honestoæ virginierat.Consultus denuo Theologus ille ordinavit pullæ, ut deferret pixidulas unguentarias exquisitorum odorum, ut moschi, ambræ, zibetti, balsami Peruviani, ac aliorum compositorum; quod cum fecisset, deambulanti per viridarium puellæ apparuit Incubus faci minaci, ac fuerenti; non tamen ad illam approximavit, sed digitum sibi momordit tanquam meditans vindictam; tandem disparuit, nec amplius ab ea visus fuit.

fumigation in the room. A new vessel, made of glass-like earth, was accordingly brought in, and filled with sweet cane, cubeb seed, roots of both aristolochies, great and small cardamon, ginger, long-pepper, caryophyleæ, cinnamon, cloves, mace, nutmegs, calamite storax, benzoin, aloes-wood and roots, one ounce of triasandalis, and three pounds of half brandy and water; the vessel was then set on hot ashes in order to force up the fumigating vapour, and the cellwas kept closed. As soon as the fumigation was done, the Incubus came, but never dared enter the cell ; only, if the maiden left it for a walk in the garden or the cloister, he appeared to her, though invisible to others and throwing his arms round her neck, stole or rather snatched kisses from her, to her intense disgust. At last, after a new consultation, the Theologian prescribed that she should carry about her person pills made of the most exquisite perfumes, such as musk, amber, chive, Peruvian balsam, and others. Thus provided, she went for a walk in the garden, where the Incubus suddenly appeared to her with a threatening face, and in a rage. He did not approach her, however, but, after biting his finger as if meditating revenge, disappeared and was never more seen by her.

72. Alia historia est, quod in Conventu Magnæ Cartusiæ Ticinensis, fuit quidam Diaconus, nomine dictus Augustinus, maximas, ac inauditas, et pene incredibiles sustinens a quodam Dæmone vexationes; quæ tolli nullo remedio spirituali (quamvis plura juxta plures exorcitas, qui liberationem, sed incassum tentarunt, fuissent adhibita) potuerunt. Me consuluit illius Conventus vicarius, qui curam divexati, utpote Clerici, ex officio habebat. Ego videns frustanea fuisse consueta exorcismorum remedia, exemplo historæ suprarecensitæ consului suffimentum simile superiori, utque divexatus pixidulas odoramentorum supradictas deferret; et quia tabacchi usum habebat, et aqua vitæ delectabatur, suasi ut et tabaccho et aqua vitæ moschata uteretur. Dæmon illi apparebat diu noctuque ultra alias species, puta scheleti, suis, asini, Angeli, avis, modo in forma unius, modo alterius ex suis Religiosis, et semel in forma sui Prælati, nempe Prioris, qui hortatus est

72. Here is the other story. In the great Carthusian Friary of Pavia there lived a Deacon, Austin by name, who was subjected by a certain Demon to excessive, unheard of and scarcely credible vexations; although many exorcists had made repeated endeavours to secure his riddance, all spiritual remedies had proved unavailing. I was consulted by the Vicar of the convent, who had the cure of the poor clerk. Seeing the inefficacy of all customary exorcisms, and remembering the above-related instance, I advised a fumigation like unto the one that has been detailed, and prescribed that the Deacon should carry about his person fragrant pills of the same kind ; moreover, as he was in the habit of using tobacco, and was very fond of brandy, I advised tobacco and brandy perfumed with musk. The Demon appeared to him by day and by night, under various shapes, as a skeleton, a pig, an ass, an Angel, a bird; with the figure of one or other of the Friars, once even with that of his own Abbot or Prior, exhorting him to keep his conscience clean, to trust in God, to confess frequently; he persuaded him to let him hear his sacramental confession, recited with him the psalms Exsurgat Deus and Qui habitat, and the Gospel according

vexatum ad puritem conscientæ, ad confidentiam in Deum, et ad frequentiam confessionis; suasit ut sibi sacramentalem confesssionem faceret, quod etiam fecit ; et expost Psalmos Exsurgat Deus et Qui habitat, et mox Evangelium S. Joannis simul sum vexato recitavit, et ad ea verba Verbum caro factum est genuglexit, et accepta stola, quæ in cella erat, et aspergillo aquæ benedictæ benedixit cellæ, ac lecto vexati, et ac si revera fuisset ipsius Prior præceptum fecit Dæmoni, ne auderet illum suum subditum amplius divexare, et post hæc disparuit, sicque prodidit quisnam esset : aliter vexatus illum suum Prælatum esse reputaverat. Postquam igitur suffimentum, ac odores, ut supra dictum est, consulueram, non distitit Dæmon juxta solitum apparere ; imo assumpta figura vexati fuit ad cameram Vicarii, et ab eo petiit aquam vitæ, ac tabaccum moschatum, dicens sibi talia valde placere. Vicarius utrumque illi dedit : quibus acceptis disparuit in momento, quo facto congnovit Vicarius se fuisse illusum a Dæmone tali pacro : quod magis confirmavit assertum vexati, qui cum juramento affirmavit, se illa die nullo modo fuisse in cella Vicarii. Iste mihi totum retulit, et ex tali facto conjeci Dæmonem illum non fuisse aqueum, to St John : and when they came to the words Verbum caro factum est, he bent his knee, and taking hold of a stole which was in the cell, and of the Holy-water sprinkle, he blessed the cell and the bed, and, as if he had really been the Prior, enjoined on the Demon not to venture in future to molest his subordinate ; he then disappeared, thus betraying what he was, for otherwise the young deacon had taken him for his Prior. Now, notwithstanding the fumigations and perfumes I had prescribed, the Demon did not desist from his wonted apparitions; more than that, assuming the features of his victim, he went to the Vicar's room, and asked for some tobacco and brandy perfumed with musk, of which, said he, he was extremely fond. Having received both, he disappeared in the twinkling of an eye, thus showing the Vicar that he had been played with by the Demon ; and this was amply confirmed by the Deacon, who affirmed upon his oath that he had not gone that day to the Vicar's cell. All that having been related to me, I inferred that, far from being aqueous like the Incubus who was in love with the maiden above spoken of, this Demon was igneous, or, at the very least, aerial, since he delighted in hot substances such as ut erat Incubus, qui virginem ad coitum sollicitabat, ut dictum supra est, sed igneum, vel ad minus aereum, ex quo gaudebat vaporibus, ac odoribus, tabacco, et aqua vitæ, quæ calida sunt. Et conjecturæ vim addidit temperamentum divexati, quod erat colericum quo ad prædominium cum subdominio, tamen sanguineo. Dæmones enim tales non accedunt nisi ad eos, qui secum in temperamento symbolizant ; ex quo validatur opinio mea de illorum corporeitate. Unde suasi Vicario, ut acciperet herbas natura frigidas, ut nymphæam, hepaticam, portulacam, mandragoram, sempervivam, plantaginem, hyoscyamum, et alias similes, et ex iis compositum fasciculum fenestræ, alium ostio cellæ suspenderet; similibusque herbis, tum cameram, tum lectum divexati sterneret. Mirum dictu! comparuit denuo Dæmon, manens tamen extra cameram, nec ingredi voluit, et cum divexatus illum interrogasset, quare de more intrare non auderet, multis verbis injuriosis jactatis contra me, qui talia consulueram, disparuit, nec amplius reversus est. 73. Ex his duabus historiis apparet tales odores, et herbas resspective sua naturali virtute, nullaque interveniente vi supernaturali vapours, perfumes, tobacco and brandy. Force was added to my surmises by the temperament of the young deacon, which was choleric and sanguine, choler predominating however; for, those Demons never approach but those whose temperament tallies with their own : another confirmation of my sentiment regarding their corporeity. I therefore advised the Vicar to let his penitent take herbs that are cold by nature, such as water-lily, liver-wort, spurge, mandrake, house-leek, plantain, henbane, and others similar, make two little bundles of them and hang them up, one at his window, the other at the door of his cell, taking care to strow some also on the floor and on the bed. Marvellous to say ! The Demon appeared again, but remained outside the room, which he would not enter; and, on the Deacon inquiring of him his motives for such unwonted reserve, he burst out into invectives against me for giving such advice, disappeared, and never came again. 73. The two stories I have related make it clear that, by their native virtue alone, perfumes and herbs drove away Demons

Dæmones propulisse; unde convincitur quod Incubi patiuntur a qualitatibus materialibus, ut proinde concludi debeat, quod communicant in materia cum iis rebus naturalibus, a quibus fugantur, et ex consequenti corpore sint præditi, quod est intentum. 74. Et magis conclusio firmatur, si impugnetur sententia Doctorum supracitatorum, dicentium, Incubum abactum a Sara fuisse vi Angeli Raphaelis, non vero jecoris piscis callionymi, qualis fuit piscis a Tobia apprehensus ad ripam Tigris, ut cum Vallesio, Sacr. Philos., c. 42., scribit Cornelius a Lap. in Tob. c. 6. v. 2., § Quarto ergo : salva enim tantorum Doctorum reverentia, talis expositio manifeste adversatur sensui patenti Textus, a quo nullo modo recedendum est dummodo non sequantur absurda. En verba Angeli ad Tobiam : "Cordis ejus particulam, si super carbones ponas, fumus ejus extricat omne genus Dæmoniorum, sive a viro, sive a muliere, ita ut ultra non accedant ad eos, et fel valet ad unguendos oculos, in quibus fuerit albugo, et sanabuntur." (Tob., c. 6. v. 8. et 9.) Notetur, qæso, assertio Angeli absoluta, et without the intervention of any supernatural force; Incubi are therefore subject to material conditions, and it must be inferred that they participate of the matter of the natural objects which have the power of putting them to flight, and consequently they have a body; that is what was to be shown. 74. But, the better to establish our conclusion, it behoves to impugn the mistake into which have fallen the Doctors above quoted, such as Vallesius and Cornelius a Lapide, when they say that Sarah was rid from the Incubus by the virtue of the Angel Raphael, and not by that of the callionymous fish caught by Tobit on the banks of the Tigris. Indeed, saving the reverence due to such great doctors, such a construction manifestly clashes with the clear meaning of the Text, from which it is never justifiable to deviate, so long as it does not lead to absurd consequences. Here are the words spoken by the Angel to Tobias : "If thou puttest on coals a particle of its heart, the smoke thereof will expel all kinds of Demons, whether from man or woman, so that they shall never return, and its gall is good for anointing eyes that have whiteness, and healing them."

universalis de virtute cordis, seu jecoris, et fellis illius piscis : non enim dicit : Si pones particulas cordis ejus super carbones, fugabis omne genus Dæmoniorum, et si felle unges oculos, in quibus fuerit albugo, sanabuntur : si enim ita dixisset, congrua esset expositio, quod nempe Raphael supernaturali sua virtute illos effectus patrasset, ad quos perficiendos inepta esset applicatio fumi, et fellis : sed non ita loquitur, sed ait talem esse virtutem fumi, et fellis absolute. 75. Quæro modo, an Angelus veritatem puram dixerit de virtute rerum, an mentiri potuerit; pariter an albugo ab oculis Tobiæ senioris ablata sit vi naturali fellis piscis, aut virtute supernaturali Angeli Raphaelis? Angelum mentiri potuisse blasphemia hæreticalis est; sequitur igitur puram veritatem fuisse ab eo assertam; talis autem non esset, si omne genus Dæmoniorum non extricaretur a fumo jecoris piscis nisi addita vi supernaturali Angeli, maxime, si hæc esset causa principalis talis

(Tobit, c. 6, v. 8 and 9). Pray notice that the Angel's assertion respecting the virtue of the heart or liver and gall of that fish is absolute, universal ; for, he does not say : "If thou puttest on coals particles of its heart, thou wilt put to flight all kinds of Demons, and if thou anointest with its gall eyes that have a whiteness, they shall be healed." If he had thus spoken, I could agree with the construction that Raphael had brought about, by his own supernatural virtue, the effects which the mere application of the smoke and the gall might not have sufficed to produce : but he does not speak thus, and, on the contrary, says absolutely, that such is the virtue of the smoke and the gall. 75. It may be asked whether the Angel spoke the precise truth regarding the virtue of those things, or whether he might have lied ; and likewise, whether the whiteness was withdrawn from the eyes of the elder Tobit by the native force of the gall of the fish, or by the supernatural virtue of the Angel Raphael? To say that the Angel could have lied would be an heretical blasphemy; he therefore spoke the precise truth ; but it would no longer be so if all kinds of Demons were not expelled by the effectus, quemadmodum scribunt de hoc casu Doctores. Mentiretur absque dubio medicus qui diceret : talis herba curat taliter pleruitidem, sive epilepsiam, ut amplius non revertatur : si herba illa non curaret illas ægritudines nisi inchoate, et perfecta illarum sanatio esset ab alia herba conjuncta priori ; sic pari modo mentitus fuisset Raphael, asserens fumum jecoris extricare omne genus Dæmoniorum ita ut ultra non accedant, si talis effectus esset a fumo solum inchoate, principaliter vero, et perfecte a virtute Angeli. Præterea talis fuga Dæmonis, vel secutura erat universaliter, et semper posito jecore piscis super carbones a quoquam, vel debebat sequi in illo solummodo casu particulari, jecore incusso a juniore Tobia. Si primum, ergo oportet, quod cuicumque talem fumum per accensionem jecoris paranti, assistat Angelus qui supernaturali virtute Dæmonem miraculose abigat regulariter ; et hoc est absurdum ; ad positionem enim rei naturalis deberet regulariter sequi miraculum, quod est incongruum, et si absque Angeli operatione fuga Dæmonis non sequeretur, mentitus fuisset Raphael asserens eam esse virtutem jecoris. Si autem effectus ille sequi non debet, nisi in illo casu particulari, mentitus fuisset Angelus smoke of the liver of the fish, unless aided by the supernatural force of the Angel, and especially, if such aid was the principal cause of the effect produced, as the Doctors assert in the present case. It would doubtless be a lie if a physician should say : such an herb radically cures pleurisy or epilepsy, and if it should only begin the cure, the completion of which required the addition of another herb to the one first used ; in the same manner, Raphael would have lied when averring that the smoke of the liver expelled all kinds of demons, so that they should not return, if that result had been only begun by the smoke, and its completion had been principally due to the virtue of the Angel. Besides, that flight of the demon was either to take place universally and by any one whomsoever putting the liver of the fish on the coals, or else it was only to occur in that particular case, the younger Tobit putting the liver on. In the first hypothesis, any person making that smoke by burning the liver should be assisted by an Angel, who, through his supernatural virtue should expel the Demons miraculously and regularly at the same time ; which is absurd ; for, either words have no meaning, or a natural fact cannot be regularly followed by a miracle ;

enuncians universaliter virtutem piscis, in fugando omni Dæmoniorum genere, quod non est dicendum. 76. Ulterius albugo oculorum detracta est ab oculis Tobiæ senioris, et ipsius cæcitas senata est a virtute naturali fellis piscis illius, ut Doctores affirmant (Liran. Dyonisius ; et Seraci. apud Cornel. in Tobi., c.6. v. 9). Piscis enim Callionymus, qui vocatur Italice bocca in capo, et quo usus est Tobias, fel habet pro celeberrimo remedio ad detegendas albugines oculorum, ut scribunt concorditer Dioscorides, l. I. c. 96., Galenus, De Simpl. Medicam., Plinius, l. 32. c. 7., Aclanius, De Ver. Histor., l. 13. c. 14., et Vallesius, De Sacr. Philos., c. 47. Textus Græcus Tobiæ, c. II. v. 13., habet : "Inpersit fel super oculos patris sui, dicens : Confide, Pater ; ut autem erosi sunt, detrivit oculos suos, et disquamatæ sunt ab angulis oculorum albugines." Cum igitur eodem contextu Angelus aperuerit and, if the Demon was not put to flight without the assistance of the Angel, Raphael would have lied when ascribing that virtue to the liver. If, on the contrary, that effect was only to be brought about in that particular case, Raphael would again have lied when assigning to that fish, universally and absolutely, the virtue of expelling the Demon : now, to say that the Angel lied is not possible. 76. The whiteness was withdrawn from the eyes of the elder Tobit, and his blindness healed, through the native virtue of the gall of that same fish, as Doctors aver. In fact, that the gall of the callionymous fish, which the Italians call bocca in capo, and of which Tobias made use, is a highly renowned remedy for removing the whiteness from the eyes, all are agreed, Dioscorides, Galen, Pliny, Aclanius, Vallesius, etc. The Greek Text of Tobit, c. II, v. 13, says : "He poured the gall on his father's eyes, saying : Have confidence, father ; but, there being erosion, the old man rubbed his eyes, and the scales of the whiteness came out at the corners." Now, since, according to the same text, the Angel had disclosed to Tobias the virtue of the liver and gall of the fish, and since, through its native virtue,

Tobiæ virtutem jecoris, et fellis piscis, et hoc sua naturali virtute cæcitatem Tobiæ senioris curaverit, concludendum est, quod etiam fumus jecoris sua naturali vi Incubum fugaverit : quod concludenter confirmatur a Textu Græco, qui ad Tobiæ c. 8. v. 2., ubi Vulgata habet : "Partem jecoris posuit super carbones vivos", sic habet : "Accepit cinerem, sive prunam thimiamatum, et imposuit cor piscis, et hepar, fumumque fecit, et quando odoratus est Dæmon odores, fugit." Et textus Hebraicus ita cantat : "Percepit Asmodeus odeorem, et fugit." Ex quibus textibus apparet, quod Dæmon fugit ad perceptionem fumi, sibi contrarii, ac nocentis, non autem a virtute Angeli supernaturali. Quod si in tali liberatione Saræ ab impetitione Incubi Asmodei, ultra fumum jecoris intervenit operatio Raphaelis, hoc fuit in alligatione Dæmonis in deserto superioris Ægypti, ut dicitur c. 8. v. 3. Tobiæ; fumus quippe jecoris nequibat in tanta distantia agere in Dæmonem, aut illum alligare. Quod insevire potest pro concordia supracitatorum Doctorum (qui voluerunt Saram perfecte liberatam a Dæmone virtute Raphaelis) cum sententia, quam tuemur : dico enim, quod ipsi senserint quod perfecta curatio Saræ a Dæmone fuerit in the gall cured the elder Tobit's blindness, it must be inferred that it was likewise through its native force that the smoke of the liver put the Incubus to flight; which inference is conclusively confirmed by the Greek text, which, Tobit, c. 8, v. 2, instead of the reading in the Vulgate : "He laid a part of the liver on burning coals", says explicitly : "He took the ashes of the perfumes, and put the heart and the liver of the fish thereupon, and made a smoke therewith; the which smell when the evil spirit had smelled, he fled." The Hebrew text says : "Asmodeus smelled the smell, and fled." From all those texts it appears that the Demon took to flight on smelling a smoke which was prejudicial and hurtful to himself, and nowise from the supernatural virtue of the Angel. If, in ridding Sarah from the assaults of the Incubus Asmodeus, the operation of the smoke of the liver was followed by the intervention of Raphael, it was in order to bind the Demon in the wilderness of High-Egypt, as related, Tobit, c. 8, v. 3; for, at such a distance, the smoke of the liver could neither operate on the Demon, nor bind him. And here we have the means of reconciling our opinion with that of the above-mentioned Doctors, who ascribe to Raphael's power Sarah's alligatione ejus in deserto, quæ fuit ab Angelo, quod et nos concedimus ; sed extricatio, sive fugatio ejusdem a cubiculo Saræ fuerit a vi innativa jecoris piscis, quod nos tuemur. 77. Probatur tertio principaliter nostra conclusio de existentia talium animalium, seu de Incuborum corporeitate, ex auctoritate D. Hieronymi, in vita S. Pauli primi Eremitæ. Refert is D. Antonium iter per desertum arripuisse, ut ad visendum D. Paulum perveniret, et post nonnullas diætas itineris Centaurum reperiisse, a quo cum fuisset percontatus mensionem D. Pauli, et ille barbarum quid infrendens potius, quam proloquens, dextræ protensione manus iter D. Antonio demonstrasset, in sylvam se abdidit cursu concitatissimo. Prosecutus iter S. Abbas in quadam valle invenit haud grandem quemdam homunculum, aduncis manibus, fronte cornibus asperata, cujus extrema pars corporis in caprarum pedes desinebat. Ad ejus aspectum substitit Antonius, et timens Diaboli artes signo Santæ Crucis se munivit. Ad tale signum nec fugit, complete riddance from the Demon : for, I say with them, that the cure of Sarah was completed by the binding of the Demon in the wilderness, the deed of the Angel; which I concede; but I maintain that the deliverance properly called, that is to say, the ejection from Sarah's bed-room, was the direct effect of the virtue of the liver of the fish. 77. A third principal proof of our conclusion regarding the existence of those animals, in other words, respecting the corporeity of Incubi, is adduced by the testimony of St Hieronymus, in his Life of St Paul, the first Hermit. St Anthony, says he, set on a journey to visit St Paul. After travelling several days, he met a Centaur, of whom he inquired the hermit's abode; whereupon the Centaur, growling some uncouth and scarcely intelligible answer, shew the way with his out-stretched hand, and fled with the utmost speed into a wood. The Holy Abbot kept on his way, and, in a dale, met a little man, almost a dwarf, with crooked hands, horned brow, and his lower extremities ending with goat's feet. At the sight of him, St Anthony stood still, and fearing the arts of the Devil, comforted himself with a sign of the nec metuit homuncio ille, immo ad sanctum senem actu humili appropinquans, palamrum frustus ad viaticum quasi pacis obsides illi offerebat. Tum B. Antonius quisnam esset interrogans, hoc ab eo responsum accepit : "Mortalis ego sum, et unus ex accolis Eremi, quos vario errore delusa Gentilitas Faunos, Satyros, et Incubos vocans colit ; legatione fungor gregis mei; precamur, ut pro nobis communem Deum depreceris, quem pro salute mundi venisse cognovimus, et universam terram exiit sonus ejus." Ad quæ gaudens D. Antonius de gloria Christi conversus ad Alexandiam, et baculo terram percutiens, ait : "Veh tibi, Civitas meretrix, quæ pro diis animalia veneraris!" Hæc D. Hieronymus, qui late prosequitur hoc factum, ipsius virtutem longo comprobans sermone. 78. De hujus historæ veritate dubitare temerarium est, cum eam constanter referat SS. Ecclesiæ Doctorum maximus D. Hieronymus, de cujus auctoritate nullus Catholicus dubitabit. Addit fol. 21. 25. Notandoæ proinde veniunt illius circumstantiæ, quæ

Cross. But, far from running away, or even seeming frightened at it, the little fellow respectfully approached the old man, and tendered him, as a peace offering, dates for his journey. The blessed St Anthony having then inquired who he was : "I am a mortal," replied he, "and one of the inhabitants of the Wilderness, whom Gentility, under its varied delusions, worships under the names of Fauns, Satyrs and Incubi ; I am on a mission from my flock : we request thee to pray for us unto the common God, whom we know to have come for the salvation of the world, and whose praises are sounded all over the earth." Rejoicing at the glory of Christ, St Anthony, turning his face towards Alexandria, and striking the ground with his staff, cried out : "Woe be unto thee, thou harlot City, who worshipest animals as Gods!" Such is the narrative of St Hieronymus, who expatiates at length on the fact, explaining its import in a long discourse. 78. It were indeed rash to doubt the truth of the above recital, constantly referred to by the greatest of the Doctors of the Holy Church, St Hieronymus, whose authority no Catholic will never deny. Let us therefore investigate the circumstances sententiam nostram evidentissime confirmant. 79. Primo notandum est, quod si ullus Sanctorum artibus Dæmonis impetitus fuit; si ullus diversas ejus artes nocendi calluit ; si ullus victorias, ac illustria de eodem tro phea reportavit, is fuit D. Antonius, ut constat ex ejus vita a D. Athanasio descripta. Dum igitur D. Antonius homunculum illum non tanquam Diabolum agnovit, sed animal intitulavit, dicens : Veh tibi, Civitas meretrix, quæ pro Diis animalia veneraris! convincitur, quod ille nullo modo fuit Diabolus, seu purus spiritus de cælo dejectus, ac damnatus, sed aliquod aliud animal. Et confirmatur, quia D. Antonius erudiens suos monachos, eosque animans ad metuendas Dæmonis violentias, aiebat, prout habetur in lectionibus Breviarii Romani in festo S. Antonii Abb. l. I., quæ recintatur in festo ipsius : "Mihi credite, Fratres, pertimescit Satanas piorum vigilias, orationes, jejunia, voluntariam paupertatem, misericordiam, et humilitatem ; maxime vero ardentem amorem in Christum Dominum, cujus unico Sanctissimæ Crucis signo debilitatus fugit." Dum igitur homunculus ille, contra quem D. Antonius Crucis signo se munivit, ad ejus aspectum thereof which most clearly confirm our opinion. 79. Firstly, we must observe that if ever a Saint was assailed by the arts of the Demon, saw through his infernal devices, and carried off victories and trophies from the contest, that Saint was St Anthony, as is shown by his life written by St Athanasius. Now, since in that little man St Anthony did not recognize a devil but an animal, saying : "Woe be unto thee, thou harlot City, who worshipest animals as Gods!", it is clear that it was no devil or pure spirit ejected from heaven and damned, but some kind of animal. Still more : St Anthony, when instructing his friars and cautioning them against the assaults of the Demon, said to them, as related in the Roman Breviary (Festival of St Anthony, Abbot, b. I) : "Believe me, my brethren, Satan dreads the vigils of pious men, their prayers, fasts, voluntary poverty, compassion and humility; but, above all, he dreads their burning love of our Lord Christ, at the mere sign of whose most Holy Cross he flies disabled." As the little man, against whom St Anthony guarded himself with a sign of the Cross, neither took fright nor fled, but approached the Saint confidently nec pavit, nec fugit, immo confidenter, humiliter que accessit ad eum dactalos illi offerens, signum est, illum nullo modo Diabolum fuisse. 80. Secundo notandum, quod homunculus ille dixit : Mortalis et ego sum; ex quibus verbis docemur, quod ille erat animal morti obnoxium, et proinde, quod per generationem esse accepit : spiritus enim immaterialis immortalis est, quia simplex, et ideo non accipit esse per generationem ex præjacente materia, sed per creationem ; unde nec amittit esse per corruptionem, quæ dicitur mors, sed per annihilationem tantum potest desinere esse. Quod si ille mortalem esse dixit, professus est se esse animal. 81. Tertio notandum, quod ait se cognovisse communem Deum in carne humana fuisse passum. Ex his verbis convincitur illud fuisse animal rationale : siquidem bruta nihil agnoscunt, nisi sensibile et præsens, unde ab ipsis Deus nullo modo cognosci potest. Quod si homunculus ille ait, se cum aliis suis cognovisse Deum in carne humana passum, hoc probat, quod aliquo revelante habuit notitiam de Deo, sicut etiam and humbly, offering him some dates, it is a sure sign that he was no Devil. 80. Secondly, we must observe that the little man said : "I also am a mortal", whence it follows that he was an animal subject to death, and consequently called into being through generation; for, an immaterial spirit is immortal, because simple, and consequently is not called into being through generation from preexistent matter, but through creation, and, consequently also, cannot lose it through the corruption called death ; its existence can only come to an end through annihilation. Therefore, when saying he was mortal, he professed himself an animal. 81. Thirdly, we must observe that he said he knew that the common God had suffered in human flesh. Those words show him to have been a rational animal, for brutes know nothing but what is sensible and present, and can therefore have no knowledge of God. If that little man said that he and his fellows were aware of God having suffered in human flesh, it shows that, by means of some revelation, he had nos habemus de illo fidem revelatam ; pariter que Deum carnem humanam assumpsisse, et in ea passum : quæ duo sunt articuli nostræ Fidei principales, nempe Dei unios, et trini existentia, et ipsius Incarnatio, Passio, et Resurrectio; ex quibus omnibus habetur, ut dicebam, illud fuisse animal rationale capax divinæ cognitionis, per revelationem, ut nos, et proinde pollens anima rationali, et ex consequenti immortali. 82. Quarto notandum, quod oraverit nomine omnium gregis sui, cujus legatione fungi se profitebatur, D. Antonium, ut communem Deum pro illis deprecaretur. Ex his deducitur, quod homunculus ille capax erat beatitudinis, et damnationis, et quod non erat in termino, sed in via : ex hoc enim, quod, ut supra probatum est, se prodidit rationalem, et anima immortali consequenter donatum, consequens est, quod et beatitudinis, et damnationis capax sit : hæc enim propria passio est Creaturæ rationalis, ut constat ex natura angelica, et humana. Item deducitur, quod ipse erat in via, et proinde capax meriti, et demeriti : si enim fuisset in termino, fuisset vel beatus, vel damnatus; neutrum autem potuit esse, quia orationes D. Antonii, quibus se acquired the notion of God, as we have ourselves the revealed faith. That God assumed human flesh and suffered in it, is the essence of the two principal articles of our Faith : the existence of God one and threefold, His Incarnation, Passion and Resurrection. All that shows, as I said, that it was a rational animal, capable of the knowledge of God through revelation, like ourselves, and endowed with a rational, and consequently, immortal soul. 82. Fourthly, we must observe that, in the name of his whole flock whose delegate he professed to be, he besought St Anthony to pray for them to the common God. Wherefrom I infer that little man was capable of beatitude and damnation, and that he was not in termino but in via; for, from his being, as has been shown above, rational and consequently endowed with an immortal soul, it flows that he was capable of beatitude and damnation, the proper share of every rational Creature, Angel or man. I likewise infer that he was on the way, in via, that is, capable of merit and demerit; for, if he had been at the goal, in termino, he would have been either blessed or damned. Now the could be neither the one nor the other; for, St Anthony's commendabat, ipsi nullo modo prodesse potuissent, si fuissent finaliter damnatus ; et si beatus fuisset, illis non eguisset. Quod ipsi se commendavit signum est eas sibi prodesse potuisse, et proinde ipsum fuisse in statu viæ, et meriti. 83. Quinto notandum, quod homunculus ille professus est, se esse legatum aliorum suæ speciei, dum dixit legatione fungor gregis mei, ex quibus verbis plura deducuntur. Unum est, quod homunculus ille non solus erat, unde potuisset credi monstrum raro contingens, sed quod plures erant ejusdem speciei ; tum quia simul congregati gregem faciebant ; tum quia nomine omnium veniebat : quod esse non posset si multorum voluntates in illum non convenissent. Aliud est, quod isti profitentur vitam socialem : ex quo nomine multorum unus ex ipsis missus est. Aliud est, quod quamvis dicantur habitare in Eremo, non tamen in eo fixa est eorum permanentia : siquidem cum D. Antonius in illa eremo alias non fuisset (distabat enim illa per multas dietas ab eremo D. Antonii), scire non potuerunt quisnam ille esset cujusve sanctitatis; necessarium igitur fuit, prayers, to which he commended himself, could have been of no assistance to him, if finally damned, and, if blessed, he stood in no need of them. Since he commended himself to those prayers, it shows they could be of avail to him, and, consequently, that he was on the way to salvation, in statu viæ et meriti. 83. Fifthly, we must observe that the little man professed to be delegated by others of his kind, when saying : "I am on a mission from my flock", words from which many inferences may be deduced. One is, that the little man was not alone of his kind, an exceptional and solitary monster, but that there were many of the same species, since congregating they made up a flock, and that he came in the name of all; which could not have been, had not the will of many centred in him. Another is, that those animals lead a social life, since one of them was sent in the name of many. Another again is, that, although living in the Wilderness, it is not assigned to them as a permanent abode; for St Anthony having never previously been in that desert, which was far distant from his hermitage, they could not have known who he was nor what his degree of sanctity; it was quod alibi eum cognoverint, et ex consequenti extra desertum illum vagaverint. 84. Ultimo notandum, quod homunculus ille ait esse ex iis, quos cæco errore delusa Gentilitas Faunos, Satyros et Incubos appellant; et ex his verbis convincitur nostrum intentum principale, Incubos nempe esse animalia rationalia beatitatis, et damnationis capacia. 85. Talium homuncionum frequens est apparitio in metallorum fodinis, ut scribit Gregorius Agricola, lib. De Animal. subterran., prope finem. Isti nempe coram fossoribus minerarum comparet induti habitu, qualem habent fossores ipsi, et jocantur inter se, tripudiantque, ac rident et cachinnantur, parvosque lapides joco mittunt in metallarios, et tunc signum est, ait Auctor prædictus, optimi proventus, ac inventionis alicujus rami, aut trunci principalis arboris mineralis. 86. Tales homunculos subterraneos negat Petrus Thyræus Novesianus, lib. De Terrificatio. Noctur., c. 2., per totum, nixus argumentis sane puerilibus, quæ therefore necessary that they should have become acquainted with him elsewhere, and, consequently, that they should have travelled beyond that wilderness. 84. Lastly, we must observe that the little man said he was one of those whom the Gentiles, blinded by error, call Fauns, Satyrs and Incubi : and by these words is shown the truth of our principal proposition : that Incubi are rational animals, capable of beatitude and damnation. 85. The apparition of such little men is of frequent occurrence in metallic mines, as is written by Gregorius Agricola in his book De Animal. subterran. They appear to the miners, clothed like themselves, play and caper together, laugh and titter, and throw little stones at them for the sake of amusement : a sign, says the above-named Author, of excellent success, and of the finding of some branch or body of a mineral tree. 86. Peter Thyræus, of Neuss, in his book De Terrification. nocturn., denies the existence of such little men, and supports his denial upon the following truly puerile arguments :

sunt hæc : si darentur hujusmodi homunciones, ubinam degunt, et quænam, et ubi habent sua domicilia, qua ratione genus suum conservant, si per generationem, aut quomodo? si oriantur, et intereant, quo cibo vitam suam sustentent ; si beatitudinis, et damnationis capaces sint, et quibus mediis propriam salutem consequantur? Hæc sunt argumenta Thyræ, quibus permotus negat talem existentiam. 87. Sed viri parum cordati est negare id, quod graves Auctores, fideque digni scribunt, quodque quotidiana constat experientia. Argumenta Thryæi nec minimum cogunt, ac ea solvimus supra a n 45. et seq. Remanet solum satisfacere quætioni ubinam locorum habitent hujusmodi homunculi, seu Incubi? Ad quod dico, quod ut supra dedimus n 71. ex Guaccio, istorum alii sunt terrei, alii aquei, alii aerei, alii ignei, quorum nempe corpora, aut constant ex talium elementorum subtiliori parte, sive licet ex pluribus constent elementis, prævalet tamen in iis, aut aqua, aut aer pro ipsorum natura. Mansiones igitur, et domicilia eorum erunt in elemento illo cujus natura in eorum corporibus prævalet : ignei enim nisi violenter, et forte nullomdo in aquis aut locis palustribus given such little men, says he, where do they live, how and where do they dwell? How do they keep up their kind, through generation or otherwise? Are they born, do they die, with what food do they sustain themselves? Are they capable of beatitude and damnation, and by what means do they procure their salvation? Such are the arguments upon which Thyræus relies for denying that existence. 87. But it really shows little judgment in a man, to deny that which has been written by grave and credible Authors, and confirmed by every day experience. Thyræus's arguments are worthless and have been already refuted, Nrs 45 and following. The only question which remains to be answered is this : where do those little men, or Incubi, dwell? To that I reply : as has been shown above (Nr 71), according to Guaccius, some are earthly, some aqueous, some aerial, some igneous, that is to say, that their bodies are made of the most subtle part of one of the elements, or, if of the combination of many elements, that yet there is one which predominates, either water or air, according to their nature. Their dwellings will consequently be found in that element which is prevalent in their morabuntur, cum hæc sint sibi contraria, nec aquei ad superiorem ætheris partem ascendere poterunt ob sibi repugnantem regionis illius subtilitatem, quod etiam videmus accidere hominibus, qui ad quorumdam Alpium summa juga pervenire nequeunt præ summa aeris subtilitate, quæ homines crassiori aeri assuetos nutrire nequit. 88. Pluribus sanctorum Patrum auctoritatibus, quas congerit Molina in p. p. D. Thom., q. 50., ar. I. circa med., probare possemus Dæmonum corporeitatem ; quæ tamen stante determinatione Concilii Lateranensis de incorporeitate Angelorum, ut dictum fuit supra n 37., exponi debent de Dæmonibus istis Incubis, ac viatoribus adhuc, non autem de Damnatis. Tamen ne nimis longus sim, solius D. Augustini, summi Ecclesiæ Doctoris, auctoritates damus, quibus evidenter convincitur illum fuisee in sententia quam nos docemus. 89. D. Augustinus igitur, lib. 2. super Genesim ad litteram c. 17. de Dæmonibus, bodies : igneous Incubi, for instance, will only stay forcibly, may be will not stay at all, in water or marshes, which are adverse to them ; and aqueous Incubi will not be able to rise into the upper part of ether, the subtlety of which region is repugnant to them. We see the like happen to men who, accustomed to thicker air, cannot reach certain lofty ridges of the Alps where the air is too subtle for their lungs. 88. Many testimonies of Holy Fathers, gathered by Molina, in his Commentary of St Thomas, would go to prove the corporeity of Demons; but, taking into account the above-quoted decision of the Council of Lateran (Nr 37), concerning the incorporeity of Angels, we must understand that the Holy Fathers had in view those Incubi Demons which are still on the way to salvation, and not those that are damned. However, to make matters short, we merely give the authority of St Austin, that eminent Doctor of the Church, and it will be clearly seen how thoroughly his doctrine harmonizes with ours. 89. St Austin, then, in his Commentary on Genesis, book 2, ch. 17, writes as follows sic habet : "Quædam vera nosse, partim quia subtiliore sensus acumine, partim quia subtilioribus corporibus vigent," et lib. 3. C. I., "etsi Dæmones aerea sunt animalia, quoniam corporum aereorum natura vigent." Et Epistola 115. ad Hebridium affirmat, eos esse "animantia aerea, seu ætherea acerrimi sensus." Et de Civit. Dei lib. II. c. 23., affirmat "Dæmonem pessimum habere corpus aereum." Et lib. 21. c. 10. scripsit : "Sunt sua quædam etiam Dæmonibus corpora, sicut doctis hominibus visum est, ex isto aere crasso et humido." Et lib. 17. c. 23. ait "se non audere definire, an Angeli corpore aereo, ita corporati possint etiam hanc pati libidinem, ut quomodo possint, sensitibus fæminis misceantur." Et in Enarrat in Psal. 85. ait "corpora beatorum futura post resurrectionem, qualia sunt corpora Angelorum ;" ei in Enarrat. in Psal. 45. ait "corpus Angelicum inferius esse anima." Et lib. De Divinit. Dæmonum, passim per totum, maxime c. 23.docet "Dæmones subtilia habere corpora." 90. Potest etiam sententia nostra auctoritatibus concerning Demons : "They have the knowledge of some truths, partly through the more subtle acumen of their senses, partly through the greater subtilty of their bodies", and, book 3, ch. I : "Demons are aerial animals, because they partake of the nature of aerial bodies." In his Epistle 115 to Hebridius, he affirms that they are "aerial or ethereal animals, endowed with very sharp senses." In the City of God, book 11, ch. 13, he says that "the worst Demon has an aerial body". Book 21, ch. 10, he writes : "The bodies of certain Demons, as has been believed by some learned men, are even made of the thick and damp air which we breathe." Book 15, ch. 23 : "He dares not define whether Angels, with an aerial body, could feel the lust which would incite them to communicate with women." In his commentary on Psalm 85, he says that "the bodies of the blessed will, after resurrection, be like unto the bodies of Angels;" Psalm 14, he observes that "the body of Angels is inferior to the soul." And, in his book De Divinit. Dæmonum, he every-where, and especially ch. 23, teaches that "Demons have subtle bodies". 90. Our doctrine can also be confirmed

Sacræ Scripturæ comprobari, quæ licet ab Expositoribus aliter declarentur, non incongrue tamen ad nostrum intentum possunt aptari. Prima est Psalmi 77., v. 24. et 25., ubi habetur : panem Angelorum manducavit homo, panem coeli dedit eis. Hic loquitur David de Manna, qua cibatus fuit Populus Israel toto tempore quo peregrinus fuit in deserto. Quærendum ergo venit, quo sensu Manna dici possit panis Angelorum. Scio quidem plerosque Doctores exponere hunc passum in sensu mystico, aientes in Manna figuratam esse Sacram Eucharistiam, quæ vocatur panis Angelorum, quia Angeli fruuntur visione Dei, qui per concomitantiam in Eucharistia reperitur. 91. Sed hæc expositio aptissima est quidem, et quam amplectitur Ecclesia in officio Sanctissimi Corporis Christi, sed in sensu spirituali est. Ego autem quæro sensum litteralem : neque enim in illo Psalmo David loquitur prophetice de futuris, sicut facit in aliis locis, ut proinde facile non sit sensum litteralem habere ; sed loquitur historice de præteritis. Ille enim Psalmus, ut patet legenti, est pura anacephalestis, seu compendium omnium beneficiorum, by the testimony of the Holy Scriptures, which, however diversely construed by commentators, are yet capable of adaptation to our proposition. First, Psalm 77, v. 24 and 25, it is said : "The Lord had given them of the bread of heaven; man did eat angels' food." David here alludes to Manna, which fed the People of Israel during the whole time that they wandered in the wilderness. It will be asked in what sense it can be said of Manna that it is the Bread of Angels. I am aware that most Doctors construe this passage in a mystical sense, saying that Manna figures the Holy Eucharist, which is styled the bread of Angels, because Angels enjoy the sight of God who, by concomitance, is found in the Eucharist. 91. A most proper construction assuredly, and which is adopted by the Church in the office of the Most Holy Body of Jesus-Christ; but it is in a spiritual sense. Now, what I want, is the literal sense; for, in that Psalm, David does not speak, as a prophet, of things to be, as he does in other places where a literal sense is not easily to be gathered; he speaks here as a historian, of things gone by. That Psalm, as is evident to whoever reads it, is a pure quæ contulit Deus Populo Hebræo ab egressu ipsius de Ægypto, usque ad tempus Davidis, et in eo versu loquitur de Manna Deserti, ut proinde quæratur quomodo, et quo sensu Manna vocetur Panis Angelorum. 92. Scio alios, Lyran., Euthim., Belarm., Titelman., Genebrard., in Psal. 77. v. 24. et 25., interpretari Panem Angelorum Panem ab Angelis paratum, seu Angelorum ministerio a Cælo demissum ; Hugonem autem Cardinalem Panem Angelorum exponere : quia ille cibus hoc efficiebat in Judæis, quod in Angelis efficit cibus illorum, pro parte : Angeli enim non incurrunt infirmitatem. Voluerunt enim expositores Hebræi, ut etiam asseverat Josephus, quod Judæi in Deserto vescentes manna, nec senescerent, nec ægrotarent, nec lassarentur; proinde illa esset tanquam panis, quo vescuntur Angeli, qui nec senio, nec ægritudine, nec lassitudine unquam laborant. 93. Istas quidem expositiones recipere æquum est, utpote tantorum Doctorum aucthoritate suffultas. Facessit tamen difficultatem, quod ministerio Angelorum anacephalæosis, or summing up of all the benefits conferred by God on the Hebrew People from the exodus from Egypt to the days of David, and the Manna of the Wilderness is spoken of in it ; how, and in what sense is it styled the Bread of Angels? that is the question. 92. I am aware that others look upon the Bread of Angels as bread prepared by Angels, or sent down from Heaven by the ministry of Angels. But Cardinal Hugo explains that qualification by saying that that food partly produced the same effect upon the Jews, which the food of Angels produces upon the latter. Angels, in fact, are not liable to any infirmity ; on the other hand Hebrew commentators, and Josephus himself, assert that whilst in the Wilderness, living upon Manna, the Jews neither grew old, nor sickened, nor tired; so that Manna was like unto the bread that Angels feed upon, who know neither old age, nor sickness, nor fatigue. 93. These interpretations should indeed be received with the respect due to the authority of such eminent Doctors. There is however one difficulty in this : that, by the

Hebræis non minus parata fuere columna nubis, et ignis coturnices, et aqua de petra, quam manna; nec tamen ista dicta fuere columna, aqua aut potus Angelorum. Cur ergo potius vocari deberet manna, quia parata ministerio Angelorum, Panis Angelorum, quam Potus Angelorum aqua eorumdem ministerio saxo educta? Insuper in sacra Scriptura panis dum dicitur panis alicujus, dicitur panis ejus qui illo vescitur, non ejus qui illum parat, aut fabricat, et de hoc infinita habemus exempla in sacra Scriptura : ut Exod. c. 23. v. 25. Benedicam panibus tuis, et aquis; lib. 2. Reg. c. 12. v. 3. De pahe illius comedens; Tob. c. 4, v. 17. Panem tuum cum egenis comede; et v. 18. Panem tuum super sepulturam Justi constitue; Ecclesiast. c. II.v. I. Mitte panem tuum super transeuntes aquas; Isai. c. 58. v. 7. Frange esurienti panem tuum; Jerem. c. II. v. 19. Mittamus lignum in panem ejus; Matth. c. 15. v. 26. Non est bomum sumere panem filiorum ; Luc. c. II. v. 3. Panem nostrum quotidianum. Ex quibus locis patenter habetur, quod panis dicitur ejus qui eo vescitur,non vero, qui ipsum conficit, affert, aut parat. Commode igitur in loco citato Psalmi accipi potest Panis Angelorum, cibus quo vescuntur Angeli non ministry of Angels, the pillars of the cloud and fire, the quails, and the water from the rock were provided for the Hebrews, no less than the Manna ; and yet they were not styled the pillar, the water or the beverage of Angels. Why therefore should Manna be called Bread of Angels, because provided by their ministry, when the qualification Beverage of Angels is not given to the water drawn from the rock likewise by their ministry? Besides, in Holy Scripture, when it is said of bread that it is the bread of somebody, it is always the bread of him who feeds on it, not of him who provides or makes it. Of this there are numberless instances : thus, Exodus, ch. 23, v. 25: "That I may bless thy bread and thy water ;" Kings, book 2, ch. 12, v. 3 : "Eating of his bread;" Tobit, ch. 4, v. 17 : "Give of thy bread to the hungry," and v. 18 : "Pour out thy bread on the burial of the Just;" Ecclesiasticus, ch. 11, v. 1 : "Scatter thy bread over the flowing waters;" Isaiah, ch. 58, v. 7 : "Deal thy bread to the hungry;" Jeremiah, ch. 11, v. 19 : "Let us put wood into his bread;" Matthew, ch. 15, v. 26 : "It is not meet to take the children's bread;" Luke, ch. 11, v. 3 : "Our daily bread." All those passages clearly show that, in Scripture, the quidem incorporei (isti enim materiali cibo non egent), sed corporei, ista nempe rationalia animalia, de quibus hucusque disseruimus, degentia in aere, et quæ ratione tenuitatis suorum corporum, ac rationalis naturæ, quam maxime ad Angelos immateriales accedunt, ut proinde nuncupentur. 94. Ducor, quia cum animalia sint, et ideo generabilia et corruptibilia, egent cibo, ut restauretur substantia corporea, quæ per effluvia deperditur ; vita enim sentientis non consistit nisi in motu partium corporearum quæ fluunt, ac refluunt, acquirntur, ac deperduntur, ac iterum reparantur ; quæ reparatio fit per substantias spirituosas, materiales tamen, attractas a vivente, tum per aeris inspirationem, tum par fermentationem cibi, per quam sustantia illius spiritualizatur, ut rationatur doctissimus Ettmullerus, Instit. Medic. Physiolog., c. 2.

bread of somebody is the bread of him who feeds upon it, not of him who makes, brings or provides it. In the passage of the Psalm we have quoted, Bread of Angels may therefore easily be taken to mean the food of Angels, not incorporeal indeed, since these require no material food, but corporeal, that is to say of those rational animals we have discoursed of, who live in the air, and, from the subtlety of their bodies and their rationality, approximate so closely to immaterial Angels as to fall under the same denomination. 94. I deduce that, being animals, consequently reproducible through generation and liable to corruption, they require food for the restoration of their corporeal substance wasted by effluvia : for the life of every sensible being consists in nothing else but the motion of the corporeal elements which flow and ebb, are acquired, lost and recruited by means of substances spirituous, yet material, assimilated by the living thing, either through the inhalation of air, or by the fermentation of food which spiritualizes its substance, as shown by the most learned Ettmuller (Instit. Medic. Physiolog., ch. 2).

95. Quia autem eorum corpus tenue est, tenui pariter, et subtili eget alimento. Hinc est quod sicut odoribus aliisque substantiis vaporosis, ac volatilibus suæ naturæ contrariis læduntur ac fugantur, ut constat ex historiis recitatis supra, n 71. et 72., ita paribus rebus sibi convenientibus delectantur, et aluntur. Porro "manna non est aliud, quam halitus aquæ, terræque, solis calore exacte attenuatus et coctus, a frigore secutæ noctis in unum coactus, densatusque," ut scribit Cornelius ; manna dico, quam demissam de cælo comederunt Hebræi, quæ toto c lo differt a manna nostrate, quæ in medicinis adhibetur ; nam hæc, ut scribit Ettmullerus Schroder. Dilucid. Physiolog., c. I. de Manna, fol. m. 154., "nihil aliud est, quam succus quarumdam arborum tenuis, vel earum transsudatio, quæ nocturno tempore permixta cum rore, matutino tempore superventu caloris solis coagualtur, et inspissatur." Manna autem Hebræorum diversis orta principiii calore solis non coagulabatur, sed vice versa liquefiebat, ut patet ex Scriptura, Exod. c. 16. v. 22. Manna ergo Hebræorum utpote constans ex halitibus tenuibus terræ et aquæ, profecto tenuissimæ erat substantiæ, utpote, quæ a sole solvebatur, et disparebat ; optime ergo

95. But, their body being subtile, equally subtile and delicate must be its food. And, just as perfumes and other vaporous and volatile substances, when adverse to their nature, offend and put them to flight, as testified by what we related above (Nrs 71 and 72), in the like manner, when agreeable, they delight in and feed upon them. Now, as is written by Cornelius, "Manna is nothing but an emanation of water and earth, refined and baked by the heat of the sun, and then coagulated and condensed by the cold of the following night;" of course, I am speaking of the Manna sent down from Heaven for the nourishment of the Hebrews, and which differs all in all from nostrate or medicinal manna : the latter, in fact, according to Ettmuller (Dilucid. Physiol., ch. I), "is merely the juice or transudation of certain trees which, during the night, gets mixed up with dew, and, the next morning, coagulates and thickens in the heat of the sun." The manna of the Hebrews, on the contrary, derived from other principles, far from coagulating, liquefied in the heat of the sun, as is shown by Scripture, Exodus, ch. 16, v. 22. The manna of the Hebrews was therefore undoubtedly of a most subtile substance, consisting as it did of emanations of earth

potuit esse talium animalium cibus, ita ut diceretur a David Panis Angelorum. 96. Alia auctoritas habetur in Evangelio Joannis, in quo, Johannes, c. 10. v. 16., ita dicitur : Alias oves habeo, quæ non sunt ex hoc ovili, et illas oportet me adducere, et vocem meam audient, et fiet unum ovile, et unus Pastor. Si quæramus quænam sint oves, quæ non sunt ex hoc ovili, et qualenam sit ovile de quo loquitur Christus Dominus, respondent communiter Expositores unum ovile Christi esse Ecclesiam, ad quam perducendi erant per prædicationem Evangeli Gentiles, qui erant oves alterius ovilis, ab ovili Hebræorum : opinantur enim Synagogam esse Christi ovile, quia dicebat David, Psal. 94. v. 9 : Nos populus ejus et oves pascuæ ejus; et quia Messias promissus fuerat Abraham et David oriturus ex eorum semine, et a populo Hebræo expectatus, et a Prophetis qui Hebræi erant vaticinatus, et ejus adventus, conversatio, passio, mors et resurrectio ir sacrificiis, cultu, et ceremoniis Hebræorum legis erant præfigurata.

and water, and being dissolved by the sun and made to disappear : consequently, it may very well have been the food of the animals we are speaking of, and thus have been truly called by David Bread of Angels. 96. We have another authority in the Gospel according to St John, ch. 10, v. 16, where it is said : "And other sheep I have, which are not of this fold : them also I must bring, and they shall hear my voice, and there shall be one fold and one shepherd." If we inquire what are those sheep which are not of that fold, and what the fold of which the Lord Christ speaketh, we are answered by all Commentators that the only fold of Christ is the Church to which the preaching of the Gospel was to bring the Gentiles, sheep of another fold than that of the Hebrews. They are, in fact, of opinion that the fold of Christ was the Synagogue, because David had said, Psalm 95, v. 7: "We are the people of his pasture, and the sheep of his hand", and also because Abraham and David had been promised that the Messiah should be born of their race, because he was expected by the Hebrew people, foretold by the Prophets who were Hebrews, and that his

97. Sed salva semper Sanctorum Patrum, ac aliorum Doctorum reverentia, non videtur talis expositio ad plenum satisfacere. Habemus enim quod de fide est a principio mundi Ecclesiam Fidelium extitisse unam, usque ad finem sæculi duraturam. Cujus Ecclesiæ caput est mediator Dei et hominum Christus Jesus, cujus contemplatione creata sunt universa, et omnia per ipsum facta. Fides enim unius Dei Trini (quamvis non ita explicite), et Verbi Incarnatio revelata fuit primo homini, et ab ipso edocti ejus filii, et ab iis descendentes. Hinc est quod quamvis plerique homines ad idolatriam deflexerint, ac veram fidem deseruerint, multi tamen veram fidem a patribus sibi traditam retinuerunt, et legem naturæ servantes in vera Ecclesia Fidelium permanserunt, ut observat Cardinalis Toletus in Job, c. 10. v. 16., et apparet in Job, qui inter Gentiles Idolatras sanctus fuit. Quamvis autem Deus populo Hebræo speciales favores contulerit, peculiaremque legem, ac ceremonias illi præscripserit, ac a Gentilibus segregaverit, non

advent, his acts, his passion, death and resurrection were prefigured in the sacrifices, worship and ceremonials of the Hebrew law. 97. But, saving always the reverence due to the Holy Fathers and other Doctors, that explanation does not seem quite satisfactory. For it is an article of belief that the Church of the Faithful has been the only one in existence from the beginning of the world, and will thus endure to the end of time. The head of that Church is Jesus-Christ, the mediator between God and men, by whose contemplation all things were made and created. Indeed, the faith in the divine Trinity, though less explicitly, and the Incarnation of the World were revealed to the first man, and by him taught his children, who, in their turn, taught them their descendants. And thus, although most men had strayed into idolatry and deserted the true faith, many kept the faith they had received from their fathers, and observing the law of nature, stayed in the true Church of the Faithful, as is noticed by Cardinal Tolet in reference to Job, who was a saint among idolatrous Gentiles. And, although God had conferred especial favours upon the Hebrew people, prescribed tamen ad eam legem Gentes tenebantur, nec fideles Hebræi aliam Ecclesiam constituebant ab Ecclesia Gentilium, qui fidem unius Dei et Messiæ venturi profitebantur. 98.Hinc est, quod etiam ex Gentilibus fuere, qui Chrisi adventum, et alia Christianæ fidei dogmata prophetarunt, ut patet de Balaam, Mercurio Trismegisto, Hydaspe, ac Sibyllis, de quibus loquitur Lactantius, lib. I. c. 6., ut scribit Cardinalis Baronius in Apparatu Annal. n 18. Et quod Messias erat a Gentilibus expectatus habet Isaias in pluribus locis, et luculentum testimonium de hoc est prophetia Patriarchæ Jacob de Messia, quæ sic ait, Gen. c. 49. v. 10 : Non auferetur sceptrum de Juda, et dux de femore ejus, donec veniat qui mittendus est, et ipse erit expectatio Gentium. Item Prophetia Aggæi, c. 2. v. 8 : Movebo omnes Gentes, et veniet desideratus cunctis gentibus, quem locum explicans Cornelius a Lap. in Aggæ. c. 2. v. 8 § Denique gentes, ait : "Gentes ante Christum credentes in Deum lege naturæ, æque ac Judæi expectabant ac desiderabant Christum." Pariter Christus ita se for them peculiar laws and ceremonials, and separated them from the Gentiles, yet those laws were not obligatory on the Gentiles, and the faithful Hebrews did not constitute a Church different from that of the Gentiles who professed their faith in one God and the coming of the Messiah. 98. And thus it came to pass that even among the Gentiles there were some who prophesied the advent of Christ and the other dogmas of the Christian faith, to wit Balaam, Mercurius Trismegistus, Hydaspes, and the Sibyls mentioned by Lactantius, book I, ch. 6, as written by Baronius, Apparat. Annal., n0 18. That the Messiah was expected by the Gentiles is shown by many passages of Isaiah, and plainly testified by the prophecy of Jacob, the Patriarch, thus worded, Genesis, ch. 49, v. 10 : "The sceptre shall not depart from Judah, nor a lawgiver from between his feet, until Shiloh (he who is to be sent) come, and unto him shall the gathering of the people be." -- Likewise in the prophecy of Haggai, ch. 2, v. 8 : "I will shake all Nations, and the desire of all Nations shall come" ; which passage is thus commented by Cornelius a Lapide : "The Gentiles before the advent of Christ, prodidit, et manifestavit Gentibus, sicut Judæis : si enim in ipsius nativitate per Angelum ejus notitia data fuit Pastoribus, per stellam miraculosam ad sui adorationem vocavit Magos, qui cum essent Gentiles fuerunt primitæ Gentium in Christo agnoscendo, et adorando, ut ait S. Fulgentius, Sermon. 6. de Epiph., sicut Pastores fuerunt primitiæ Judæorum. Itidem manifestatio adventus Christi per prædicationem (non quidem Apostolorum) prius facta est Gentilibus, quam Jud is ; siquidem ut scribit Ven. Mater Soror Maria de Agrede, in Vita J. C. Et B. M. V., p. I. l. 4. c. 26. N. 664 : "Quando B. M. Virgo cum S. Joseph portavit Puerum Jesum in Ægyptum, fugiendo Herodis persecutionem, mansit ibi per septennium : quo tempore ipsa Beatissima Virgo prædicavit Ægyptiis veri Dei fidem, et Filii Dei in carne humana adventum." Ulterius in Christi nativitate multa fuere prodigia non solum in Judæa, sed in Ægypto, ubi corruerunt idola, ac oracula conticuere; Romæ, ubi fons olei scaturiit; visus globus aurei coloris de cælo in terram descendere ; apparuere tres soles; ac contra naturam circulus variegatus ad modum iridis solis discum circumscripsit ; in Græcia, ubi oraculum Delphicum obmutuit, et interrogatus Apollo ab who believed in God and observed the law of nature, expected and desired Christ equally with the Jews." Christ himself disclosed and manifested himself to the Gentiles as well as to the Jews; for, at the same time as the Angel apprized the shepherds of his nativity, by means of the miraculous star he called the Magi to worship him, who, being Gentiles, were the first among the Nations, as the shepherds among the Jews, to acknowledge and worship Christ (Vide St Fulgentius, Sermon 6, upon Epiphany). In like manner, the advent of Christ was made known by preaching (I am not speaking of the Apostles) to the Gentiles before it was to the Jews. As is written by the Venerable Mother, Sister Maria of Agreda, in her Life of Jesus-Christ and the Blessed Virgin Mary : "When the Blessed Virgin Mary, fleeing with St Joseph, from the persecution of Herod, carried the Infant Jesus into Egypt, she tarried there seven years; and, during that time, the Blessed Virgin herself preached to the Egyptians the faith of the true God and the advent of the Son of God in human flesh." Besides, the nativity of Christ was attended by numerous prodigies, not only in Judæa, but also in Egypt, where the idols tumbled and the

Augusto ipsi sacrificante in proprio palatio, ubi eidem aram extruxerat, de causa silentii suii, respondit, ut referunt Nicephorus, l. I c. 17., Suisdas, verbo Augustus, et Cedrenus, Compend. Histor.: Me puer Hebræeus, Divos Deus ipse gubernans, Cedere sede jubet, tristemque redire sub orcum; Aris ergo dehinc tacitis abscedito nostris. Et multa alia acciderunt prodigia, quibus prænunciabatur Gentilibus Filii Dei adventus, quæ ex variis Aucthoribus recitat Baronius, Apparat. Annal. Eccles. n 24. et seq., et Cornelius in Aggæ. c. 2. v. 8. 99. Ex istis patet, quod etiam Gentiles pertinebant ad ovile Christi idem, ad quod spectabant Judæi, puta ad Ecclesiam eamdem fidelem; igitur non potest recte dici, quod illa verba Christi : Aliaas oves habeo, quæ bib sunt ex hoc ovili, accipienda sint de Gentilibus, qui communem cum Hebræis oracles were hushed ; in Rome, where a spring of oil gushed out, a gold-coloured globe was seen to descend from the skies on earth, three suns appeared, and an extraordinary ring, variegated like a rainbow, encircled the disc of the sun; in Greece, where the oracle of Delphi was struck dumb, and Apollo, asked the reason of his silence by Augustus, who was offering up a sacrifice in his own palace where he had raised an altar to him, answered : "A Hebrew child, who sways the Gods, and himself a God, Bids me quit my seat and return to the infernal regions; Depart therefore from our altars, henceforward mute." There were many more prodigies warning the Gentiles of the advent of the Son of God : they have been collected from various Authors, by Baronius, and are to be found in his Apparat Annal. Eccles., and Cornelius, Commentary upon Haggai. 99. From all this it is clear that the Gentiles also belonged, like the Jews, to the fold of Christ, that is, to the same Church of the Faithful; it cannot therefore be correctly said that the words of Christ : "Other sheep I have, which are not of this fold", are applicable to the Gentiles, who habuerunt de Deo fidem, de Messia spem, prophetiam, expectationem, et signa, et prædicationem. 100. Dico igitur quod nomine aliarum ovium commode possunt intelligi Creaturæ istæ rationales, sive animalia, de quibus hucusque disseruimus. Cum enim, ut diximus, capaces sint beatitudinis, et damnationis, et Christus Jesus sit mediator Dei, et hominum, immo totius rationalis creaturæ (creaturæ enim rationales, quæ beatitudinem consequuntur, hanc obtinent intuitu meritorum Christi per ab eo sibi collatam gratiam, sine qua nequit beatitudo obtineri), debuit omnis rationalis creatura de eo venturo spem habere, sicut de uno Deo fidem, et de ipsius in carne nativitate, et de præceptis legis gratiæ manifestationem. Istæ igitur erant oves, quæ non erant ex hoc ovili humano, et quas adducere Christum oportebat, et quæ ejus vocem nempe notitiam de ipsius adventu, et de evangelica doctrina, quantum per se, tum per Apostolos Christus erat manifestarus, audire debebant, et ex iis ac hominibus in cælo beatificatis fieri unum ovile, et unus Pastor.

had, in common with the Hebrews, the faith in God, the hope, prophecy, expectation, prodigies and preaching of the Messiah. 100. I therefore say that by the words other sheep may very well be understood those rational Creatures or animals of whom we have been treating hitherto. They being, as we have said, capable of beatitude and damnation, and Jesus-Christ being the mediator between God and man, as also every rational Creature (for rational creatures attain to beatitude in consideration of the merits of Christ, through the grace he confers upon them, without which beatitude is impossible of attainment), every rational creature must have cherished, at the same time as the faith in one God, the hope of the advent of Christ, and have had the revelation of his nativity in the flesh and of the principles of the law of grace. Those were therefore the sheep which were not of that human fold, and which Christ had to bring; the sheep which were to hear His voice, that is, the announcement of His advent and of the evangelical doctrine, either directly through Himself, or through the Apostles ; the sheep which, partaking with men of heavenly beatitude, were to realize one fold and one shepherd.

101. Huic expositione quam incongruam non puto, vim addit id quod supra n 77. ex D. Hieronymo retulimus de homunculo illo qui rogavit D. Antonium, ut communem Deum, quem in carne humana esse passum cognoverat, pro se et suis deprecaretur. Innuitur enim ex his, quod illi notitiam habuerunt de adventu et morte Christi, quem tamquam Deum optabant sibi propitium, ut proinde ad hoc intercessionem D. Antonii expostularent. 102. Facit ad idem id, quod ex Eusebio de Præparat. Evang. l. 5. c. 9., et Plutarcho l. de Defectu Oracul., refert Cardianalis Baronius, Appar. Annal. n 129., et recenset inter prodigia, quæ tempore mortis Christi evenere. Recitat igitur ex citatis Aucthoribus quod Tiberii Imperatoris, sub quo passus est Christus, tempore, navigantibus nonnullis a Græcia in Italiam, circa Insulas Echinades, cessatis ventis, noctu navigium appulit prope terram. Audita fuit ab omnibus vox magna quæ vocavit Tramnum. Erat is Nauclerus navigii, quo resondente Adsum, replicavit vox : "Quando perveneris prope quandam paludem, annunciabis MAGNUM PANA MORTUUM ESSE" : quod cum Tramnus fecisset,

101. To this interpretation, which I hold to be in no way improper, force is added by what we related, according to St Hieronymus, of that little man who requested St Anthony to pray, for him and his fellows, unto the common God, whom he knew to have suffered-in human flesh. For, it implies that they were aware of the advent and of the death of Christ, whom, as God, they were anxious to propitiate, since they sought, to that effect, the intercession of St Anthony. 102. Thereto tends also the fact mentioned by Cardinal Baronius (Appar. Annal. n0 129), after Eusebius and Plutarch, as being one of the prodigies which took place at the time of the death of Christ. He relates that in the reign of the Emperor Tiberius, when Christ suffered, whilst mariners bound from Greece to Italy, were by night, and during a calm, in the vicinity of the Echinade Isles, their ship was brought close to land. All the crew heard a loud voice calling Tramnus, the master of the ship. He having answered to his name, the voice replied : "When near such a marsh, announce that the great Pan is dead." Which Tramnus having done, there arose suddenly, as from a numberless

auditi sunt repente multorum, imo multitudinis prope infinitæ gemitus, et ulutatus. Profecto isti fuerunt Dæmone, seu Angeli corporei, seu animalia rationalia prope paludem degentia, utpote aquea, quæ audita morte Christi, qui nomine magni Pan efferebatur, in lacrymas et lamenta effussa sunt ; prout etiam Hebræi nonnulli visa Christi morte percutientes pectora sua revertebantur (Luc. c. 23. v. 48). Ex hucusque igitur deductis patet, quod dantur hujusmodi Dæmones, succubi et incubi, constantes sensu, et ipsius passionibus obnoxii, ut probatum est; qui generantur, corrumpuntur, et capaces sunt beatitudinis, et damnationis, et ratione corporis subtilioris, nobiliores homine sunt, et qui si cum hominibus, maribus aut foeminis, carnaliter commiscentur, peccant, et eo peccato, quo peccat homo jugendo se cum bruto, quod est homine ignobilius; proinde non raro hi Dæmones consuetudinem habentes cum homine, aut equabus, post longam habitam communicationem eos interficiunt. Causa porro hujus est, quod si inter tales datur peccatum, cum sint in via, dari etiam debet pænitentia; sicut ergo homini peccanti consuetudinaliter cum bruto, ad tollendam occasionem recidivandi, Confessarius injungit, ut brutum multitude, groans and shrieks. Doubtless, they were Demons, or corporeal Angels, or rational animals living near the marsh on account of their aqueous nature, and who, hearing of the death of Christ, described by the name of Great Pan, burst into tears and bewailing, like some of the Jews who, after witnessing the death of Christ, went home smiting their breasts (Luke, ch. 23, v. 48). From all that has been deduced above, it is therefore clear that there are such Demons, succubi and incubi, endowed with senses and subject to the passions thereof, as has been shown; who are born through generation and die through corruption, are capable of beatitude and damnation, more noble than man, by reason of the greater subtilty of their bodies, and who, when having intercourse with man, male or female, fall into the same sin as man when copulating with a beast, which is inferior to him. Also, it not unfrequently occurs that those Demons slay the men, women or mares with whom they have had protracted intercourse; and the reason is that, being liable to sin whilst on the way to salvation, in via, they must likewise be open to repentance ; and, in the same manner as a man, who habitually sins with a beast, is enjoined by his confessor tollat de medio, ita tali Dæmoni consuetudinario in peccato, et tandem poenitenti accidit, ut animal cum quo peccavit, sive homo, sive brutum fuerit, occidat ; nec enim tali Dæmoni mors data homini peccatum erit, sicut mors data bruto non imputatur tamquam peccatum homini : ratione enim essentialis differentiæ inter Dæmonem hujusmodi, et hominem, idem erit homo Dæmoni, quod est homini brutum. 103. Scio multos, et forte plerosque, qui hæc legerent, dicturos de me, quod Epicurei et Stoici Philosophi nonnulli dixerunt de Divo Paulo, Actor. c. 17. v. 18. : Novorum Dæmoniorum videtur annunciator, et datam doctrinam exsibillabunt. Sed isti tenebuntur solvere argumenta supra posita, et dicere quinam sint Dæmones isti Incubi, vulgo Foletti, qui exorcismos, res sacras, et Christi Crucem non pavent, ac alios effectus istorum, ac phænomena salvare, quæ nos ex data doctrina ostendimus. 104. Solvitur ergo ex his, quæ hucusque deducta sunt, quæstio, quam proposuimus to destroy that beast, with a view to suppressing the occasion of relapsing, it may likewise happen that the penitent demon should slay the animal with which it sinned, whether man or beast ; nor will death thus occasioned to a man be reckoned a sin to the Demon, any more than death inflicted on a beast is imputed as a sin to man ; for, considering the essential difference between a Demon of that kind and man, the man will be the same thing to the Demon as the beast is to man. 103. I am aware that many, perhaps most of my readers, will say of me what the Epicureans and some Stoic Philosophers said of St Paul (Acts of the Apostles, ch. 17, v. 18). "He seemeth to be a setter forth of strange gods", and will deride my doctrine. But they will none the less have to answer the foregoing arguments, to show what are those Incubi Demons, commonly called Goblins, who dread neither exorcisms, nor the holy things, nor the Cross of Christ, and to explain the various effects and phenomena related when propounding that doctrine. 104. What we have hitherto deduced accordingly solves the question laid down supra n 30 et n 34 : resolutive innuimus, quomodo mulier potest ingravidari a dæmone Incubo. Non enim hoc præstare potest ex semine sumpto ab homine, ut fert communis opinio, quam confutavimus n 31 et 32 : sequitur ergo, quod ipsa imprægnatur a semine Incubi, cum enim animal sit, et generet, proprio pollet semine : et hoc modo optime salvatur generatio Gigantum secuta ex commixtione Filiorum Dei cum Filiabus hominum; nati siquidem sunt ex tali concubitu Gigantes, qui licet homini essent similes, corpore tamen erant majores : et quamvis a Dæmonibus geniti, viribus proinde pollerent, non tamen Dæmonum vires et potentiam æquabant, ut sequitur in mulis, hinnis et burdonibus, qui medii quodammodo sunt inter eas species animalium, a quibus promiscue generantur, et superant quidem imperfectiorem, non attingunt autem perfectiorem speciem generantium : mulus enim superat asinum, sed non æquat perfectionem equæ, a quibus generatur. 105. Confirmat autem hanc sententiam consideratio, quod animalia genita ex commixtione diversarum specierum non generant;

Nrs 30 and 34, to wit : how a woman can be got with child by an Incubus Demon? In fact, it cannot be brought about by sperm assumed from a man, agreeably to the common opinion which we confuted, Nrs 31 and 32; it follows, therefore, that she is directly impregnated by the sperm of the Incubus, which, being an animal and capable of breeding, has sperm of its own. And thus is fully explained the begetting of Giants from the intercourse of the Sons of God with the Daughters of men : for that intercourse gave birth to Giants who, although like unto men, were of higher stature, and, though begotten by Demons, and consequently of great strength, yet equalled them neither in might nor in power. It is the same with mules, which are intermediate, as it were, between the kinds of animals from whose promiscuousness they are sprung, and which excel indeed the most imperfect, but never equal the most perfect : thus, the mule excels the ass, but does not attain the perfection of the mare, which have begotten it. 105. In confirmation of the above inference, we observe that animals sprung from the mixing of different kinds do not sed sunt sterilia, ut patet in mulis. Gigantes autem non leguntur Gigantes generasse, sed natos a Filiis Dei, puta Incubis, et Filiabus hominum : cum enim concepti fuerint ex semine Dæmoniaco mixto cum humano, non potuerunt, tamquam mediæ speciei inter Dæmonem et generare. 106. Dicetur fortasse contra hoc, non posse, ex semine Dæmonum, quod pro sui natura oppotet esse tenuisssimum, fieri mixturam cum semine humano, quod crssum est; unde nec generatio sequi possit. 107. Respondeo quod, ut dictum fuit supra n 32 : virtus generandi consistit in spiritu, qui simul cum materia spumosa et viscida deciditur a generante; sequitur ex hoc, quod semen Dæmonis quantumvis tenuissimum, qui tamen materiale, optime potest commisceri cum spiritu materiali seminis humani, ac fieri generatio. 108. Replicabitur adhuc contra conclusionem, quod si vere fuisset Gigantum generatio ex semine Incoborum et Mulierum, breed, but are barren, as is seen with mules. Now we do not read of Giants having been begotten by other Giants, but of their having been born of the Sons of God, that is Incubi, and the Daughters of men : being thus begotten of the Demoniac sperm mixed with the human sperm, and being, as it were, an intermediate species between the Demon and man, they had no generative power. 106. It may be objected that the sperm of Demons, which must, by nature, be most fluid, could not mix with the human sperm, which is thick, and that, consequently, no generation would ensue. 107. I reply that, as has been said above, Nr 32, the generative power lies in the spirit that comes from the generator at the same time as the spumy and viscous matter; it follows that, although most liquid, the sperm of the Demon, being nevertheless material, can very well mix with the material spirit of the human sperm, and bring about generation. 108. It will be retorted that, if the generation of Giants had really come from the combined sperms of Incubi and Women, nunc quoque Gigantes nascerentur : non desunt enim mulieres coeuntes cum Incubis, ut patet ex gestis SS. Bernardi et Petri de Alcantara, et aliarum historiarum, quæ passim ab auctoribus recitantur. 109. Respondeo, quod prout ex Guaccio dictum fuit supra n 81 : alii sunt hujusmodi Dæmones terrei, alii aquei, aerei alii, et alii ignei, qui respective in propriis eorum elementis habitant. Videmus autem animalia eo majora esse quo majus est elementum in quo degunt, ut patet in piscibus, inter quos licet multi sint minuti, ut etiam sunt plura animalia terrestria minutissima, et tamen quia elementum aquæ majus est elemento terræ (utpote continens majus semper est contento), ideo pisces a tota specie superant in magnitudine molis animalia terrestria, ut patet in balenis, orcynis, pistis seu pistricibus, thynnis, ac aliis piscibus cetaceis, seu viviparis, qui quodvis animal terrestre longe superant. Porro cum Dæmones hujusmodi animalia sint, ut hucusque probatum est, eo erunt majores in magnitudine quo elementum majus pro sui natura inhabitabunt. Et cum aer excedat aquam, et ignis aere major sit, sequitur, quod Dæmones ætherei ac

Giants would still be born in our time, since there is no lack of women who have intercourse with Incubi, as is shown by the Acts of St Bernard and Peter of Alcantara, and other stories related by various authors. 109. I reply that, as has been said above, Nr 81, from Guaccius, some of those Demons are earthly, some aqueous, some aerial, some igneous, and they all dwell in their respective element. Now, it is well known that animals are of larger size, according to the element they live in ; thus with fishes, many of which are diminutive, it is true, as happens with animals that live on land ; but, the element water being larger than the element earth, since the container is always larger than the contents, fishes as a species, surpass in size the animals that dwell on land, as shown by whales, tunnies, cachalots, and other cetaceous and viviparous fish which surpass by far all animals that live on land. Consequently, these Demons being animals, as has been shown, their size will be proportionate to the extent of the element they dwell in, according to their nature. And, air being more extensive than water, and fire than air, it follows that ethereal and ignei longe superabunt terrestres et aqueos, tum in mole corporis, tum in virtute. Nec contra hoc facit instantia de avibus, qui licet incolant aerem, qui major est aqua, tamen corpore minores sunt a tota specie piscibus et quadrupedibus, quia aves, licet per aerem volatu spatientur, revera tamen pertinent ad elementum terræ, in qua quiescunt ; aliter enim pisces nonnulli qui volant, ut hirundo marina, et alii, dici deberent animalia aerea, quod falsum est. 110. Advertendum autem, quod post diluvium aer iste terraqueo globo citissimus magis incrassatus est ex humiditate aquarum, quam fuerit ante diluvium, et hinc forte est, quod ex tali humido, quod est principium corruptionis, fiat, quod homines non ætatem ita producant, ut faciebant ante diluvium. Ex ista autem aeri crassitie fit, quod Dæmones ætherei, ac ignei cæteris corpulentiores, nequeunt diutius manere in hoc aere crasso, et si descendunt aliquando hoc fit violenter, et eo modo quo urinatores ad ima maris descendunt.

igneous Demons will by far surpass their earthly and aqueous fellows, both in stature and might. It would be to no purpose to instance, as an objection, birds which, although inhabitants of the air, a more extensive element than water, are smaller, as a species, than fishes and quadrupeds ; for, if birds do indeed travel through the air by means of their wings, they no less belong to the element earth, where they rest; otherwise, some fishes that fly, such as the sea swallow, would have to be classed among aerial animals, which is not. 110. Now, it must be observed that, after the flood, the air which surrounds our earthy and aqueous globe, became, from the damp of the waters, thicker than it had been before; and, damp being the principle of corruption, that may be the reason why men do not live as long as they did before the flood. It is also on account of that thickness of the air that ethereal and igneous Demons, more corpulent than the others, can no longer dwell in that thick atmosphere, and if they do descend into it occasionally, do so only by force, much as divers descend into the depths of the sea.

III. Ante diluvium autem, cum adhuc aer non ita crassus erat, veniebant Dæmones, et cum mulieribus miscebantur, et gigantes procreabant, qui magnitudinem corpoream Dæmonum generantium æmulabantur. Nunc vero ita non est : Dæmones enim Incubi, qui foeminas incessunt, sunt aquei quorum corporis moles magna non est : et proinde in forma homuncionum apparent, et quia aquei etiam salacissimi sunt; luxuria enim in humido est : ut proinde Venerem e mari natam Poetæ finxerit, quod Mythologi explicant de libidine, quæ oritur ab humiditate. Cum ergo Dæmones, qui corpore parvi sunt his temporibus mulieres imprægnent, non gigantes, sed staturæ ordinariæ filii nascuntur. Sciendum porro quod si miscentur corporaliter cum mulieribus Dæmones in sua ipsorum corpulentia naturali, nulla facta immutatione aut artificio, muliere illos non vident, nisi tanquam umbram pæne incertam, ac quasi insensibilem, ut patet in muliere illa, de qua diximus supra n 28., quæ osculabatur ab incubo, cujus tactus vix ab ea sentiebatur. Quando vero volunt se visibiles amaiis reddere, atque ipsis delectationem in congressu carnali afferre, sibi indumentum visible assumunt, et corpus crassum reddunt. Qua vero hoc

III. Before the flood, when the air was not yet so thick, Demons came upon earth and had intercourse with women, thus procreating Giants whose stature was nearly equal to that of the Demons, their fathers. But now it is not so : the Incubi Demons who approach women are aqueous and of small stature; that is why they appear in the shape of little men, and, being aqueous, they are most lecherous. Lust and damp go together : Poets have depicted Venus as born of the sea, in order to show, as explained by Mythologists, that lust takes its source in damp. When, therefore, Demons of short stature impregnate women nowadays, the children that are born are not giants, but men of ordinary size. It should, moreover, be known that when Demons have carnal intercourse with women in their own natural body, without having recourse to any disguise or artifice, the women do not see them, or if they do, see but an almost doubtful, barely sensible shadow, as was the case with the female we spoke of, Nr 28, who, when embraced by an Incubus, scarcely felt his touch. But, when they want to be seen by their mistresses, atque ipsis delectationem in congressu carnali afferre, they assume a visible disguise and a palpable arte fiat, ipsi norunt. Nobis curta nostra Philosophia hoc non pandit. Unum scire possumus, et est, quod tale indumentum seu corpus ex solo aere concreto constare nequiret, hoc enim esse deberet per condensationem, et proinde per frigus; unde oporteret, quod corpus illud ad tactum esset veluti glacies, et ita in coitu mulieres non delectaret, sed torqueret, cum tamen contrarium eveniat. 112. Visa igitur differentia Dæmonum spiritualium, qui cum sagis coeunt, et Incuborum, qui cum foeminis minime sagis rem habent, perpedenda est gravitas hujus criminis in utroque casu. 113. In coitu sagarum cum Dæmonibus, eo quia non fit nisi cum apostasia a Fide, et Diaboli cultu, et tot aliis impietatibus quas recensuimus supra a n 12. ad 24., est maximum quorumque peccatorum, quæ ab hominibus fieri possunt : et ratione tantæ enormitatis contra Religionem, quæ præsupponitur coitu cum Diabolo, profecto Dæmonialitas maximum est criminum carnalium. Sed spectato delicto carnis ut sic, et ut abstracto a peccatis body. By what means this is effected, is their secret, which our short-sighted Philosophy is unable to discover. The only thing we know is that such disguise or body could not consist merely in concrete air, since this must take place through condensation, and therefore by the influence of cold; a body thus formed would feel like ice, et ita in coitu mulieres non delectaret, but would give them pain ; and it is the reverse that takes place. 112. Being admitted the distinction between spiritual Demons, which have intercourse with witches, and Incubi, who have to do with women that are nowise witches, we have to weigh the grievousness of the crime in both cases. 113. The intercourse of witches with Demons, from its accompanying circumstances, apostasy from the Faith, worshiping of the Devil, and so many other ungodly things related above, Nrs 12 to 24, is the greatest of all sins which can be committed by man; and, considering the enormity against Religion which is presupposed by coition with the Devil, Demoniality is assuredly the most heinous of all carnal crimes. But, taking the sin of contra Religionem, Dæmonialitas redigenda est ad simplicem pollutionem. Ratio, et quidem convicentissima, est quia Diabolus, qui rem habet cum sagis, purus spiritus est, et est in termino ac damnatus ut dictum supra fuit; proinde si cum sagis coit, hoc facit in corpore assumpto, aut a se formato, ut sentiunt communiter Theologi. Porro corpus illud quamvis moveatur , non tamen vivens est ; sequitur ergo quod coiens cum tali corpore, sive mas sive f mina fuerit, idem delictum committit, ac si cum corpore inanimato aut cadavere coiret, quod esset simplex mollities, ut alias demonstravimus. Verum est, quod ut observavit etiam Cajetanus, talis coitus effective potest habere deformitates aliorum criminum juxta corpus a Diabolo assumptum, et vas : si enim assumeret corpus virginis consanguineæ, aut sacræ, effective esset tale crimen incestus aut sacrilegium, et si in figura bruti coiret, aut in vase præpostero, evaderet Bestialitis aut Sodomia. II4. In coitu autem cum Incubo, in quo the flesh as such, exclusive of the sins against Religion, Demoniality should be reduced to simple pollution. The reason is, and a most convincing one, that the Devil who has to do with witches is a pure spirit, has reached the goal and is damned, as has been said above; if, therefore, he copulates with witches, it is in a body assumed or made by himself, according to the common opinion of Theologians. Though set in motion, that body is not a living one; and it follows that the human being, male or female, coiens cum tali corpore, is guilty of the same offence as if copulating with an inanimate body or a corpse, which would be simple pollution, as we have shown elsewhere. It has, moreover, been truly observed by Cajetanus, that such intercourse can very well carry with it the disgraceful characteristics of other crimes, according to the body assumed by the Devil, and the part used : thus, if he should assume the body of a kinswoman or of a nun, such a crime would be incest or sacrilege ; if coition took place in the shape of a beast, or in vase præpostero, it would be Bestiality or Sodomy. 114. As for intercourse with an Incubus, nulla habetur qualitas, vel minima, criminis contra Religionem, difficile est rationem invenire, per quam tale delictum Bestialitate et Sodomia gravior esset. Siquidem gravitas Bestialitatis præ Sodomia, prout supra diximus, consistit in hoc, quod homo vilificat dignitatem suæ speciei jungendose cum bruto quod est speciei longe inferioris sua. In coitu autem cum Incubo diversa est ratio : nam Incubus ratione spiritus rationalis, ac immortales, æqualis est homini; ratione vero corporis nobilioris, nempe subtilioris, est perfectior, et dignior homine; et hoc modo homo jungens se Incubo non vilificat, immo dignificat suam naturam, et ita, juxta hanc considerationem, Dæmonialitas nequit esse gravior Bestialitate. 115. Tamen gravior communiter censetur, et ratio, meo videri, potest esse : quia peccatum contra Religionem est, quævis communicatio cum Diabolo, sive ex pacto, sive non ; puta habendo cum eo consuetudinem aut familiaritatem, seu ab eo petendo auxilium, consilium, favorem, aut ab ipso quærendo revelationem futurorum, relationem præteritorum, absentium, wherein is to be found no element, not even the least, of an offence against Religion, it is hard to discover a reason why it should be more grievous than Bestiality and Sodomy. For, as we have said above, if Bestiality is more grievous than Sodomy, it is because man degrades the dignity of his kind by mixing with a beast, of a kind much inferior to his own. But, when copulating with an Incubus, it is quite the reverse : for the Incubus, by reason of his rational and immortal spirit, is equal to man ; and, by reason of his body, more noble because more subtle, he is more perfect and more dignified than man. Consequently, when having intercourse with an Incubus, man does not degrade, but rather dignifies his nature; and, taking that into consideration, Demoniality cannot be more grievous than Bestiality. 115. It is, however, commonly held to be more grievous, and the reason I take to be this : that it is a sin against Religion to hold any communication with the Devil, either with or without compact, for instance by being habitually or familiarly connected with him, by asking his assistance, counsel or favor, or by seeking from him the revelation of things to be, the knowledge of aut alias occultorum. Hujusmodi autem homines, seu mulieres, concumbendo cum Incubis, quos nesciunt animalia esse, sed putant esse diabolos, contra conscientiam erroneam delinquunt ; et hoc modo ex conscientia erronea ita peccant cum Incubis se jungendo, ac si cum diabolis coirent : unde et gravitatem ejusdem criminis incurrunt.

FINIS

things gone by, absent, or otherwise hidden. Thus, men and women, by mixing with Incubi, whom they do not know to be animals but believe to be devils, sin through intention, ex conscientia erronea, and their sin is intentionally the same, when having intercourse with Incubi, as if such intercourse took place with devils; in consequence, the grievousness of their crime is exactly the same.

FINIS

APPENDIX

The manuscript of Demoniality breaks off with the conclusion just given. In a purely philosophical and theoretical acception, the work is complete : for it was enough that the author should define, in general terms, the grievousness of the crime, without concerning himself with the proceedings which were to make out the proof, nor with the penalty to be inflicted. Both those questions, on the contrary, had, as a matter of course, a place assigned to them in the great work De Delictis et P nis, which is a veritable Code for the Inquisitor ; and Father Sinistrari of Ameno could not fail to treat them there with all the care and conscientiousness he has so amply shown in the foregoing pages. The reader will be happy to find here that practical conclusion to Demoniality. (Note by the Editor.)

PROBATIO DÆMONIALITATIS SUMMARIUM I. De probatione criminis Dæmonialitatis, distinquendum est. 2. Indicia probantia coitum Sagæ cum Diabolo. 3. Requiritur confessio ipsius malefici ad plenam probationem. 4. Historia de Moniali habente consuetudinem cum Incubo. 5. Si adsint indicia visa in recitata historia, potest ad torturam deveniri. I. Quantum ad probationem hujus criminis attinet, distinguendum est de Dæmonialitate, puta, vel ejus, quæ a Sagis seu Maleficis fit cum Diabolis ; sive de ea, quæ ab aliis fit cum Incubus.

PROOF OF DEMONIALITY SUMMARY 1. Distinctions to be made in the proof of the crime of Demoniality. 2. Signs proving the intercourse of a Witch with the Devil. 3. The confession of the Sorcerer himself is requisite for a full eviction. 4. Tale of a Nun who had an intimacy with an Incubus. 5. If the indictment is supported by the recitals of eye-witnesses, torture may be resorted to. 1. As regards the proof of that crime, a distinction must be made of the kind of Demoniality, to wit : whether it is that which is practiced by Witches or Wizards with the Devil, or that which other persons perpetrate with Incubi.

2. Quoad primam, probato crimine pacti facti cum Diabolo, probata remanet Dæmonialitas ex consequentia necessaria; nam scopus tum Sagarum, tum Maleficorum in ludis nocturnis, ultra convivia, et choreas, est hujusmodi infamis congressus : aliter, illius criminis nullus potest esse testis, quia Diabolus, qui Sagæ visibilis est, aliorum oculos effugit. Verum est, quod aliquoties visæ sunt mulieres in sylvis agris, et nemoribus, supinæ jacentes, ad umbilicum tenus denudatæ, et juxta dispositionem actus venerei, devaricatis et adductis cruribus, clunes agitare, prout scribit Guacc., lib. I, cap. 12, v. Sciendum est sæpius, fol. 65. Tali casu emergeret suspicio vehemens talis criminis, dummodo esset aliunde adminiculata, et crederem talem actum per testes sufficienter probatum, sufficere Judici ad indagandam tormentis veritatem; et hoc maxime, si post aliqualem moram in illo actu, visus fuisset a muliere elevari quasi fumus niger, et tunc mulierem surgere, prout ibidem scribit Guaccius; talis enim fumus, aut umbra, Dæmonem fuisse concumbentem cum foemina inferre potest. Sicut etiam, si mulier visa fuisset concumbere cum homine, qui post actum de repente evanuit, ut non semel accidisse idem auctor ibidem narrat.

2. In the first case, the compact entered into with the Devil being proved, the evidence of Demoniality follows as a necessary consequence; for, the purpose, both of Witches and Wizards, in the nightly revels that take place after feasting and dancing, is none other but that infamous intercourse; otherwise there can be no witness of that crime, since the Devil, visible to the Witch, escapes the sight of others. Sometimes, it is true, women have been seen in the woods, in the fields, in the groves, lying on their backs, ad umbilicum tenus nudatæ, et juxta dispositionem actus venerei, their legs divaricatis et adductis, clunes agitare, as is written by Guaccius, book I, chap. 12, v. Sciendum est sæpius, fol. 65. In such a case there would be a very strong suspicion of such a crime, if supported by other signs; and I am inclined to believe that such action, sufficiently proved by witnesses, would justify the Judge in resorting to torture in order to ascertain the truth; especially if, shortly after that action, a sort of black smoke had been seen to issue from the woman, and she had been noticed to rise, as is also written by Guaccius; for it might be inferred that smoke or shadow had been the Devil himself, concumbens cum

3. Cæterum ad probandum concludenter aliquem esse Maleficum, seu Maleficam, requiritur propria confessio ; nullus enim haberi potest de hoc testis, nisi forte sint alii Malefici, qui in judicio deponunt de complicibus; sed quia socii criminis sunt, eorum dictum non concludit, nec etiam ad torturam sufficit, nisi alia existent indicia, puta, sigillum Diaboli impressum in eorum corpore, prout diximus supra num. 23,; et in eorum domibus, facta perquisitione, inveniant signa, ac instrumenta artis diabolicæ, ut ossa mortuorum, præsertim calvariam ; crines artificiose contextos ; nodos plumarum intricatos ; alas, aut pedes, aut ossicula vespertilionum, aut bufonum, aut sepentium; ignotas seminum species; figuras cereas; vasculos plenos incognito pulvere, aut oleo, aut unguentis minime notis, etc., ut ordinarie contingit reperiri a Judicibus, qui, accepta accusatione de hujusmodi Sagis, ad capturam, et domus visitationem deveniunt, ut scribit Delbene,.

f mina. Likewise if, as has more than once happened, according to the same author, a woman had been seen concumbere cum homine, who, the action over, suddenly disappeared. 3. Moreover, in order to prove conclusively that a person is a Wizard or a Witch, the own confession of such person is requisite : for there can be no witnesses to the fact, unless perhaps other Sorcerers giving evidence at the trial against their accomplices; from their being confederates in the crime, their statement is not conclusive and does not justify the recourse to torture, should not other indications be forthcoming, such as the seal of the Devil stamped on their body, as aforesaid, Nr 23, or the finding in their dwelling, after a search, of signs and instruments of the diabolic art : for instance, bones and, especially, a skull, hair artfully plaited, intricate knots of feathers, wings, feet or bones of bats, toads or serpents, unfamiliar seeds, wax figures, vessels filled with unknown powder, oil or ointments, etc., as are usually detected by Judges who, upon a charge being brought against Sorcerers, proceed to their apprehension and the search of their houses.

de Off. S. Inquis., par. 2. dub. 206, num.7. 4. Quantum vero ad probationem congressus cum Incubo, par est difficultas; non minus enim Incubus, ac alii Diaboli effugiunt, quando volunt, visum aliorum, ut videri se faciunt a sola amasia. Tamen non raro accidit, quod etiam visi sint Incubi modo sub una, modo sub alia specie in actu carnali cum mulieribus. In quodam Monasterio (nomen ejus et urbis taceo, ne veterem ignominiam memoriæ refricem) quædam fuit Monialis, quæ cum alia Moniali, quæ cellam habebat suæ contiguam, simultatem ex levibus causis, ut assolet inter mulieres, maxime Religiosas, habebat. Hæc sagax in observando quascumque actiones Monialis sibi adversæ, per plures dies vidit, quod ista in diebus æstivis, statim a prandio non spatiabatur per viridarium cum aliis, sed ab iis sequestra, se retrahebat in cellam, quam sera obserabat. Observatrix igitur æmulla curiositate investigans, quid tali tempore illa facere posset, etiam ipsa in in propriam cellam se recipiebat; cæpit auatem audire submissam quasi duorum insimull colloquentium vocem (quod facile erat, nam cella parvo simplicis, scilicet lateris unius,

4. The proof of intimacy with an Incubus offers the same difficulty ; for, no less than other Demons, the Incubus is, at will, invisible to all but his mistress. Yet, it has not seldom happened that Incubi have allowed themselves to be surprised in the act of carnal intercourse with women, now in one shape, now in another. In a Monastery (I mention neither its name nor that of the town where it lies, so as not to recall to memory a past scandal), there was a Nun, who, about trifles, as is usual with women and especially with nuns, had quarrelled with one of her mates who occupied a cell adjoining to hers. Quick at observing all the doings of her enemy, this neighbour noticed, several days in succession, that instead of walking with her companions in the garden after dinner she retired to her cell, where she locked herself in. Anxious to know what she could be doing there all that time, the inquisitive Nun betook herself also to her cell. Soon she heard a sound, as of two voices conversing in subdued tones, which she could easily do, since the two cells were divided but by a

disterminio dividebatur), mox sonitum poppysmatum[4], concussionis lecti, gannitus, ac anhelitus, quasi duorum concubentium ; unde aucta in æmula curiositate stetit in observatione, ut sciret, quinam in illa cella essent. Postquam autem per tres vices vidit, nullam aliam Monialem egressam e cella illa, præter æmulam, dominam cellæ, suspicata est Monialem in camera absconditum aliquem virum, clanculum introductum, retinere; unde et rem detulit ad Abbatissam, quæ consilio habito cum discretis, voluit audire sonitus, et observare indicia relata ab accusatrice, ne præcipitanter et inconsiderate ageret. Abbatissa igitur cum discretis se receperunt in cellam observatricis, et audierunt strepitus, et voces, quas accusatrix detulerat. Facta igitur inquisitione, an ulla Monialium potuisset

---

[4] Poppysmatum. -- That word being but little used, it may be useful to record here the definition given of it by the Glossarium eroticum linguæ latinæ (auctore P. P., Paris, 1826) : POPPYSMA. Oris pressi sonus, similis illi quo permulcentur equi et canes. Obscene vero de susurro cunni labiorum, quum frictu madescunt. Father Sinistrari, well versed in classical literature, had turned to account the following epigram of Martial (book VII, 18) : GALLAM Quum tibi sit facies, de qua nec f mina possit Dicere, quum corpus nulla litura notet; Cur te tam rarus cupiat, repetatque fututor, Miraris?Vitium est non leve, Galla, tibi. Accessi quoties ad opus, mixtisque movemur Inginibus, cunnus non tacet, ipsa taces. Di facerent, ut tu loquereris, et ipse taceret! Offendor cunni garrulitate tui. Pedere te mallem : namque hoc nec inutile dicit Symmachus, et risum res movet ista simul. Quis ridere potest fatui poppysmata cunni? Quum sonat hic, cui non mentula mensque cadit Dic aliquid saltem, clamosoque obstrepe cunno : Et si adeo muta es, disce vel inde loqui (Editorial Note.)

slight partition), then a peculiar friction, the cracking of a bed, groans and sighs, *quasi duorum concumbentium*; her curiosity was raised to the highest pitch, and she redoubled her attention in order to ascertain who was in the cell. But having, three times running, seen no other nun come out but her rival, she suspected that a man had been secretly introduced and was kept hidden there. She went and reported the thing to the Abbess, who, after holding counsel with discreet persons, resolved upon hearing the sounds and observing literature, had turned to account the following epigram of Martial (book VII, 18):

secuum in illa cella clausa esse, et reperto quod non, Abbatissa cum discretis fuit ad ostium cellæ clausæ; et pulsato frustra pluries ostio , cum Monialis nec respondere, nec aperire vellet, Abbatissa minata est, se velle ostium prosterni facere, et vecte aggredi opus fecit a quadam conversa. Tunc aperuit ostium Monialis, et facta perquisitione, nullus inventus est in camera. Interrogata Monialis cum quonam loqueretur, et de causa concussionis lecti, anhelituum, etc., omnia negavit. Cum vero res perseveraret, accuratior, ac curiosior Monialis æmula perforavit tabulas lacunaris, ut posset cellam introspicere ; et vidit elegantem quemdam juvenem cum Moniali concumbentem, quem etiam eodem modo ab aliis Monialibus videndumcuravit. Delata mox accusatione ad Episcopum, ipsaque Moniali omnia negante, tandem metu tormentorum comminatorum the indications that had been denounced her, so as to avoid any precipitate or inconsiderate act. In consequence, the Abbess and her confidents repaired to the cell of the spy, and heard the voices and other noises that had been described. An inquiry was set on foot to make sure whether any of the Nuns could be shut in with the other one ; and the result being in the negative, the Abbess and her attendants went to the door of the closed cell, and knocked repeatedly, but to no purpose : the Nun neither answered, nor opened. The Abbess threatened to have the door broken in, and even ordered a convert to force it with a crow-bar. The Nun then opened her door : a search was made and no one found. Being asked with whom she had been talking, and the why and wherefore of the bed cracking, of the sighs, etc., she denied every thing. But, matters going on just the same as before, the rival Nun, become more attentive and more inquisitive than ever, contrived to bore a hole through the partition, so as to be able to see what was going on inside the cell; and what should she see but an elegant youth lying with the Nun, and the sight of whom she took care to let the others enjoy by the same adacta, confessa est se cum Incubo consuetudinem habuisse. 5. Quando igitur adessent talia indicia, sicut in recitata historia intervenerunt, posset utique in rigoroso examine rea constitui; sine tamen ejus confessione, non censendum est delictum plene probatum, quantumvis a testibus visus fuisset congressus; siquidem aliquando accidit, quod Diabolus, ut infamiam alicui innocenti pararet, præstigiose talem concubitum repræsentaverit. Unde in his casibus debet Judex Ecclesiasticus esse perfecte oculatus.

means. The charge was soon brought before the bishop : the guilty Nun endeavoured still to deny all; but, threatened with the torture, she confessed having had an intimacy with an Incubus. 5. When, therefore, indications are forth-coming, such as those recited above, a charge might be brought after a searching inquiry; yet, without the confession of the accused, the offence should not be regarded as fully proved, even if the intercourse were testified by eye-witnesses; for it sometimes happens that, in order to undo an innocent female, the Devil feigns such intercourse by means of some delusion. In those cases, the Ecclesiastical Judge must consequently trust but his own eyes.

Quantum ad poenas Dæmonialitatis, nulla lex civilis, aut canonica, quam legerim, reperitur, quæ poenam sanciat contra crimen hujusmodi. Tamen, quia crimen hoc supponit pactum, ac societam cum Dæmone, ac apostasiam a fide, ultra veneficia, atque alia infinita propemodum damna, quæ a Maleficis inferuntur, regulariter, extra Italiam, suspendio et incendio punitur. In Italia autem, rarissime traduntur hujusmodi Malefici ab Inquisitoribus Curiæ sæculari.

PENALTIES As regards the penalties applicable to Demoniality, there is no law that I know of, either civil or canonical, wich inflicts a punishment for a crime of that kind. Since, however, such a crime implies a compact and fellowship with the Demon, and apostasy of the faith, not to speak of the malefices and other almost numberless outrages perpetrated by Sorcerers, as a rule it is punished, out of Italy, by the gallows and the stake. But, in Italy, it is but very seldom that offenders of that kind are delivered up by the Inquisitors to the secular power.

BIOGRAPHICAL NOTICE[5]

Father Ludovico Maria Sinistrari, of the Order of Reformed Minors of the strict Observance of St. Francis, was born in Ameno, a small town of the district of St. Julius, in the diocese of Novara, on the 26th of February 1622. He received a liberal education and went through a course of humanities in Pavia, where, in the year 1647, he entered the Order of Franciscans. Devoting himself henceforward to tuition, he was first a professor of Philosophy ; he then, during fifteen successive years, taught Theology in the same town, amidst a numerous concourse of students attracted from all parts of Europe by his high repute. His sermons preached in the principal cities of Italy, at the same time as they caused his eloquence to be admired, were productive of the most happy results for piety. Equally endeared to the World and to Religion, he had been favoured by nature with the most brilliant gifts : square frame, high stature, open countenance, broad forehead, sparkling eyes, high-coloured complexion, pleasant conversation replete with sallies of wit[6]; more valuable still, he was in possession of the gifts of grace, through which he was enabled to sustain, with unconquerable resignation, the assaults of an arthritical disease he was subject to; he was, moreover, remarkable for his meekness, candour and absolute submission to the rules of his Order. A man of all sciences[7], he had learnt foreign languages without any master, and often, in the general Meetings of his Order, held in Rome, he supported, in public, theses de omni scibili. He, however, addicted himself more particularly to the study of Civil and Canon laws. In Rome he filled the appointment of Consulter to the supreme Tribunal of the Holy-Inquisition; was some time Vicar general of the Archbishop of Avignon, and then Theologian attached to the

---

[5] This Notice is an extract from tome I of the complete works of Father Sinistrari, Romæ, 1753.

[6] Quadrato corpore, statura procera, facie liberali, fronte spatiosa, oculis rutilantibus, colore vivido, jucundæ conversationis, ac lepidorum salium.

[7] Omnium scientiarum vir.

Archbishop of Milan. In the year 1688, charged by the general Meeting of Franciscans with the compilation of the statutes of the Order, he performed this task in his treatise entitled Practica criminalis Minorum illustrata. He died in the year of our Lord 1701, on the 6th of March, at the age of seventy-nine[8]

---

[8] The complete works of P. Sinistrari (Rome, Giannini, 1753-1754, 3 vol. in-folio) include the following books : Practica criminalis Minorum illustrata, -- Formularium criminale, -- De incorrigibilium expulsione ab Ordinibus Regularibus, -- De Delictis et P nis, to which should be added the present work : De Dæmonialitate, published for the first time in the year 1875.

LETTER OF THE REV. FATHER PROVINCIAL OF CAPUCHINS FOR THE PROVINCE OF P... P..., Friday (8 October 1875).[9]

Pax

MONS. ISIDORE LISEUX, Paris.

I have gone through the work you sent me yesterday, and have, indeed, been satisfied with the edition; the time has not yet arrived for me to give my opinion on the value of the work itself. Here you would have met with no other works of the Rev. Father Sinistrari of Ameno than his book : Practica criminalis Minorium ; De Delictis et P nis is to be found, I believe, in another of our convents; but you would have been given a most welcome reception. I believe that Des Grieux can hardly have resided in the present St-Sulpice, which dates but from the year 1816. .... So far as a superficial glance has enabled me to ascertain, there are some other mistakes ; but, altogether, the work is a good one, and you may accept of the congratulations of Your very little servant, Fr. A... o. m. c. m. p. Convent of Capuchins, rue ....

---

[9] Paris, imprimerie D. JOUAUST, rue Saint-Honoré, 338.

www.ingramcontent.com/pod-product-compliance
Lightning Source LLC
Chambersburg PA
CBHW071152160426
43196CB00011B/2060